LIFE IN
VICTORIAN LONDON

Life in
VICTORIAN
LONDON

L. C. B. SEAMAN

B. T. Batsford Ltd
LONDON

First published 1973
© L. C. B. Seaman, 1973
ISBN 0 7134 1465 0
Printed in Great Britain by
Fletcher & Son Ltd., Norwich
for the publishers
B. T. BATSFORD LTD.,
4 Fitzhardinge Street,
London W1H 0AH

Acknowledgments

The Author wishes to acknowledge the help of his wife in the final preparation of the manuscript, and to thank Mary Smith for typing many of the chapters.

The Author and Publisher would like to thank the following for the illustrations which appear in this book: Aerofilms for fig. 72; The British Museum for fig. 26; Dr Barnado's Homes for fig. 16; Fulham Reference Library for fig. 4; Greenwich Library for fig. 37; Guildhall Library for fig. 29; Hammersmith Central Reference Library for fig. 33; Kensington and Chelsea Libraries for figs. 51–54; Mrs P. H. Lee-Steere for fig. 57; J. G. Links for fig. 39; The London Museum for figs. 1, 9, 11, 12, 25, 40, 41, 45, 49, 61, 73, 77, 79; The London Museum and the daughters of G. W. Joy for fig. 24; London Transport for figs. 22, 23, 30–32, 42, 43; The Mansell Collection for fig. 18; Port of London Authority for fig. 5; Radio Times Hulton Picture Library for fig. 58; Royal Holloway College for fig. 15; The Science Museum for fig. 27; The Wellcome Institute for fig. 50; Victoria and Albert Museum for figs. 21 (Crown copyright), 70, 74, 76; Westminster Public Library for fig. 81. Fig. 55 is from the author's collection.

The quotations from *Notes on England, 1872* by Hippolyte Taine, translated by Edward Hyams, 1957, are printed by permission of Thames and Hudson Ltd. The map of London's railways, fig. 20, is based on Bacon's Popular Atlas of the British Isles, 1896.

Contents

The Illustrations

Introduction

Full-scale academic histories of Victorian London as a whole are still few and far between and even such partial studies as exist are of fairly recent vintage. Accordingly, in spite of the multitude of books about Victorian social conditions and about various aspects of Victorian London, there have been fewer firm guide-lines to assist me in the writing of this book than might be expected. Furthermore, the expression 'Life in Victorian London' is a form of shorthand which may too easily obscure the realisation that it can refer to all sorts and conditions of men and women spending their lives in all sorts of living and working conditions over a period of sixty-four years of continuous and rapid change; and doing so in a sprawling accumulation of expanding yet always congested communities within a very large area without accurate geographical or administrative boundaries. Such considerations make generalisations almost impossible.

For this reason I have chosen wherever possible to be specific rather than general and to concentrate on some of the major facets of London life rather than risk extreme superficiality by trying to deal with all of them. I have tried to examine those features of London life that were either peculiar to it or which it had in common with other great capital cities. Peculiar to it were its topography and the developing transport system without which it could not have become at once a great sprawl but still recognisably 'London'. Peculiar to it also were its confused administrative systems and its fascinating suburban variety. Characteristic of it, because it was a vast metropolis, were those features which gave it its status as a 'Great Babylon' as well as a 'Great Wen'. It is of the nature of a metropolis that it is a place to which people go in search of recreation and entertainment, of sin and sensation and of wonderful things to buy. Equally typical of very large cities are overcrowding and squalor, co-existing with wealth, fashion and opulence. I hope, however, I have said enough, in addition to this, to make it clear that London was also, like any other great city in the British Isles, a place where thousands of quite ordinary people made themselves homes and earned their daily bread.

Woking 1973   L.C.B.S.

8

I

London Surveyed:
1837 and After

The impression London made upon the visitor in the early
Victorian period was not unlike the impression he might have
received a century later: one of size, sprawl and congestion.
It would seem, as it still does, a place of infinite contrasts and
surprises. It contained beautiful buildings but was not itself
beautiful. Its existence was undeniable, but its limits indefinable, and its extent greater than the mind could take in;
so that for its inhabitants, perhaps even more than for the
visitor, large parts of it were always unknown. Not merely was
it forever sprawling towards outlying villages to turn them into
suburbs; the villages themselves expanded towards the
tentacles that reached out to embrace them. And always there
was change, so that large sections of it were continually being
made unrecognisable to the elderly who had known those
areas in their childhood and early manhood. If the main agents
of visual change in the half-century or so before Victoria's
reign had been developments planned by the crown, the
aristocracy and the City Corporation, the railways, all through
the Queen's reign, were to shatter and reshape the urban scene
like a succession of minor earthquakes.

In size alone, London always astonished. It had, for hundreds
of years before Victoria, been the largest centre of population
in the world outside China and India. In the early nineteenth
century it had twice as many inhabitants as Paris, 4 times as
many as Vienna, 6 times as many as Berlin. The first census of
the Victorian period, that of 1841, showed that, since 1801,

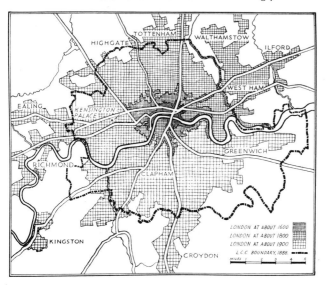

The expansion of London 1800–1900; note the limited area assigned to the London County Council

its population had doubled from around 1 million to well over 2 million. This rate of growth was below that of the new industrial towns of the North and Midlands, exploding with the consequences of the early Industrial Revolution. The populations of Glasgow, Manchester and Liverpool had increased roughly 4-fold, Birmingham's 3-fold, Bradford's 5-fold. Moreover, whereas, in 1801, London had been the only urban centre in the British Isles with more than 100,000 inhabitants, by 1841, Birmingham, Bristol, Sheffield all exceeded that figure and Glasgow, Liverpool and Manchester had populations of over a quarter of a million inhabitants.

As the decades passed, though it was never again, as it had been in 1801, to be over 12 times larger than the second largest town in the kingdom, by the time of the Queen's death in 1901, London's population had increased from the 2,239,000 of 1841 to 6,586,000, and was still 7 times larger than Glasgow, over 8 times larger than Birmingham and about ten times as large as Liverpool or Manchester. And if its rate of growth in the early years of the century had been less spectacular than that of the industrial towns, it was explosive in Victorian times, bearing in mind that it had grown hardly at all in the first half of the eighteenth century.

The growth of London's population was due partly to natural increase and partly to continuous immigration all through the reign from all the southern counties. Some of this rural immigration contributed to the initial expansion of the outer suburbs. Irish immigration was stimulated by the Great Famine of the late 1840s; and continental immigration, particularly into the East End, by political and racial persecution in eastern Europe. The continuous arrival in London of poor rural and foreign immigrants, many of them unskilled, was a contributory cause of the low wages, the unemployment and the crowded living conditions in the inner areas of the metropolis to which so many newcomers were attracted because it was there that the greatest opportunities for unskilled labour were to be found.

London also constituted the largest single market for consumer goods in the world and this contributed not only to the success of the new factories created in the north and midlands by the Industrial Revolution but also to the steady growth of manufacturing industry in London itself. By mid-Victorian times, London contained no less than 15 per cent of all workers in England and Wales employed in manufacturing industries. Most worked in small-scale concerns operating in the inner suburbs. Crowded Clerkenwell had its highly skilled clock-, watch- and instrument-makers. Bermondsey, like neighbouring Southwark, was a busy centre of the leather and tanning trades.

An important London industry: Barclay's Brewery, Southwark, 1843

Brewing was a major industry, with important breweries in Southwark, Spitalfields and Pimlico. The south-western suburbs produced nearly half the country's supply of vinegar. Flour mills and biscuit-making flourished in Bermondsey and Rotherhithe, sugar-refining in Stepney. New industrial areas developed north of the river in Victorian times: the production of jute, soap and matches in Bow and Hackney and of chemicals at Stratford; the gas industry established itself in Beckton, and tar-processing was carried on at Silvertown.

At the beginning of the reign, London was still important for mechanical engineering. It was in engineering workshops originally established in Lambeth by Henry Maudslay in 1810 that some of the most famous Victorian engineers had received their early training, among them James Nasmyth, inventor of the steam hammer, and Joseph Whitworth. Until the 1860s, the high quality of London engineering ensured that the ship-yards at Limehouse, Blackwall, Millwall and Rotherhithe played a notable part in the building of iron ships. By 1870, however, the Thames-side shipping industry had collapsed, partly because both labour and raw materials could be obtained more cheaply on the Clyde and the Tyne. By that date, London had also ceased to be a great engineering centre.

London's only textile industry was silk weaving, carried on in Spitalfields and Bethnal Green. Particularly prosperous in the first quarter of the century, with wages fixed by local magistrates and their products protected by a ban on imported silk fabrics, the silk weavers had been deprived of both advantages by 1826. Undercut thereafter by the foreigner and the new provincial silk factories, the London weavers were already in a sorry plight by the time Victoria came to the throne. Whereas many of them had once been prosperous and respectable, by the 1840s the most skilful weaver, even with the aid of his wife and children could, working 12 or more hours a day, often earn little more, after deduction of expenses, than between 9s (45p) and 10s (50p) a week. The weavers' living conditions, particularly in Bethnal Green, were notoriously bad, and they and their families easily fell victim to cholera.

In mid-Victorian times, nearly 6 per cent of all London males and over 8 per cent of all females were employed in work connected with clothing; only production and distribution of food employed more men and domestic service more women; a quarter of all clothing workers in England and Wales were Londoners. Bespoke tailoring was carried on mainly in the West End; early in Victorian times the East End, originally concerned mainly with the secondhand clothes business, became the centre of the wholesale ready-made clothing industry. The major processes in tailoring could be done by fairly simple machinery, a fact which explained the multiplicity of small businesses; most work in the trade was farmed out by middlemen or, as they were usually described, 'sweaters', to individuals or to small groups working in squalid, cramped and ill-ventilated rooms which remained outside the scope of factory legislation almost to the end of the reign. Tailoring was thus a 'sweated' trade in the two senses that working conditions were deplorable and the pay for long hours of work exceedingly low. Most male tailors worked as individuals, taking work from 'sweaters' in cheap ready-made

Girls in a West End dressmakers' as depicted in a working men's magazine. The hour is five past midnight and restoratives are administered to stave off exhaustion.

tailoring, or 'slopwork' as it was called, and earning perhaps a mere 13s (65p) a week. To buy a sewing machine would increase earnings only temporarily: the relative cheapness of this device constantly forced rates of pay downwards. Women and girls employed in dressmaking in West End establishments might work from 12 to as many as 17 hours a day; wages, according to skill, ranged from a fairly high rate of £25 a year down to as low as 6s (30p) a week. The work was so arduous that by their mid-thirties dressmakers looked, it was said, 10 years older than the average domestic servant. The less skilful among them ended up where the more unfortunate began, in the ready-made slop trade in the East End, perhaps sewing buttons by hand. Here, the rate paid by the sweaters could fall to as low as 5s (25p) a week for a 12-hour day.

The supply and distribution of food constituted the largest single occupation for male Londoners. At the beginning of the reign sheep and cattle were driven live to the London markets and it was not until the end of the reign that the bulk of London's meat was transported to the capital in carcass form by rail or steamship. Similarly, in early Victorian times, fruit and vegetables were brought to Covent Garden in carts from the 15,000 acres of market gardens to be found within a 10-mile radius of the central area and thence distributed by cart or on foot to retail markets and shops. This system, employing vast numbers in heavy work of a most monotonous kind, was later to be much changed by the coming of the railways. Milk was provided (to be used for cooking rather than for drinking) by outer-suburban cowkeepers who brought it to the centre by cart, or by cowkeepers who kept their beasts in an inner-suburban backyard. The distribution to householders was done by men and women carrying 10-gallon tubs borne on a yoke slung across their shoulders. It was not until the 1870s that milk brought to London by rail began to end the activities of the cowkeepers.

This selection of occupations shows how London's size generated the multiplicity of occupations designed to serve its need for food and drink and clothing. To these must be added the large numbers employed in domestic service, those continuously employed in the building trades, in the ever-expanding transport system, in the transport of coal by sea for a large part of the reign, and of course the dockworkers in the great Port of London. As the administrative centre of a populous kingdom and an ever-growing empire, and as the financial capital of the world, London also contained an exceptionally large number of persons working in the public service, in banking and insurance, and in the expanding professions. The growth of insurance and banking and the sophisticated financial skills of the City of London ministered to the needs of commerce and industry in all 5 continents in Victorian times. Moreover, all through the reign, the cost of Britain's imports was always well in excess of the value of the commodities the country exported; the favourable balance of payments the country enjoyed derived from the profits made by the 'invisible exports' such as shipping services, banking and insurance, the greater part of which was organised from London. The contribution to the prosperity of the whole of Victorian England by this specialised service emanating from London can hardly be over-emphasised.

The office workers in the banks, in the legal and insurance offices and the offices of the railway companies all belonged by definition to the middle classes since they were neither trades-people nor manual workers. An income of £300 a year, which represented, for example, the net income of the average family doctor, was held to be the absolute minimum for the maintenance of genuinely middle-class standards of living; but most even of London's lower middle class earned less than that. Junior clerks might earn £80 to begin with and might expect to rise eventually to a salary of £200 a year. Few clerks ever achieved higher wages and many of them did not earn much more than the best-paid skilled artisan. The average wage of engine drivers, skilled instrument-makers and cabinet-makers was about 35s (£1.75) a week or about £90 a year.

This helps to explain why the long streets of small terrace houses in the suburbs could house either lower middle-class or 'superior' working-class families. It helps too, to explain the cult of respectability, quite as potent a social force among the mass of Londoners as in other parts of the country. Lower middle-class people had to be as respectable as possible since their financial superiority to the skilled manual worker was often only marginal; the prosperous artisan class had to be as respectable as possible in order to assert that they were every bit as 'good as' their supposed betters. Nobody could safely claim to be middle class who did not employ at least one domestic servant; but the most comfortably-off artisan family might blur class distinction still further by having similar aspirations.

Yet, for all its status as a great manufacturing and mercantile city, London had taken only the most timid steps towards the development of a centralised administration and the creation of a sense of civic pride before the establishment of the London County Council in 1888; indeed, with the creation of the Metropolitan Boroughs in 1899, it may perhaps be said to have taken 28 steps away from corporate identity. This was the most bewildering fact about London; not only could one not define its geographical limits; neither could one discover its administrative centre. It had neither, or rather, it nearly always had several of both.

The 'wooden bridge in faraway Fulham' with a wintry view of Putney parish church in 1881

This administrative and geographical shapelessness of London was its principal inheritance from the pre-Victorian centuries and one of its legacies to the twentieth century. The head of state had for some time been accustomed to live at Windsor, of which one could at least assert that it was certainly not in London; and only in 1762 had the crown acquired (and under George IV renovated) Buckingham House and turned it into a royal residence, a fact which did not prevent St James's Palace remaining the nominal source from which royal Orders in Council were issued and to which foreign ambassadors were accredited. Nor were the effective seats of power, the Palace of Westminster, Downing Street, and a still rudimentary Whitehall, officially the heart of London, except colloquially; and this despite the fact that building developments since the late seventeenth century had already linked it on the northern bank of the Thames with the historic City of London and, on a somewhat narrow front, with Southwark on the bedraggled south bank. The City of Westminster had its own identity and was in a state of reciprocated hostility with the City of London.

The 600 acres of the City of London proper, stretching from the Temple to the Tower, was a jealously-guarded and complicatedly-governed preserve, furiously opposed on principle to any attempt from Westminster either to get it to govern properly or to let anybody encroach on its right to evade its civic responsibilities; or on its pretensions to control everything that went on in its environs. The City had, for example, vigorously opposed the building of Westminster Bridge in the 1740s: both because it might detract from London Bridge, the only other bridge across the Thames eastwards of a wooden bridge at faraway Fulham, and because the City had jurisdiction over the Thames from the Medway to as far upstream as Staines and therefore regarded the project as an intrusion by the state upon its privileges.

Owing to the enormous wealth of its leading citizens, the City of London had been a decisive factor in bringing about the downfall of the Stuarts and the consequent Glorious Revolution of 1688. England's system of government which had, during the eighteenth century, emerged from that event, had therefore depended to a large extent on the initial support it had received from City merchants. Lacking as it did any wide basis of popular support, the Hanoverian political system had survived very largely by interfering as little as possible with entrenched institutions, privileges and corporations, for it was for doing precisely that that the Stuarts had been cast aside.

The City therefore continued to be governed by an extremely complex medieval system presided over by the Lord Mayor and his two Sheriffs. There was a small, exclusive and exceedingly wealthy Court of Aldermen, from whose number the four City MPs were drawn, and who acted as the City's Justices of the Peace. There were also the Court of Common Council, the Court of Common Hall and the Court of Wardmote. Of these, Common Council had become the most important administrative body in the City. Hardly less important than these cumbersome and forever quarrelsome bodies were the ancient City Guilds or Companies. They were very wealthy and used their wealth lavishly to bribe (or as they would have preferred to say 'influence') all who might be of use to them in preserving or increasing their wealth and privilege. Nevertheless, since every ratepayer in the City had some say in the election of one or other of the City's Councils, and admission into a Company as a freeman (and thereafter, on further payment, to the status of liveryman) was not very difficult, there was, relative to the situation elsewhere, a large measure of ratepaying democracy in the early Victorian City. This in itself excited a complacent unwillingness to admit that anything need be changed, and a niggling refusal to accept responsibility for any matters outside the City boundaries which might involve expense. Similarly the entrenched 'ratepayer mentality' of the City's democracy could at times be more resistant even than that of the new industrial towns towards incurring expenditure on necessary public works.

Outside the City boundaries, the inner suburbs were left to shift for themselves and were subject to the City's attentions only if they sought to encroach upon the City's privileges and profits (by, for instance, setting up their own markets). The unit of administration was the parish, whose public affairs were managed by parish vestries. Not until after 1831 did it gradually become usual for these vestries to be elected by ratepayers and even so, in many London parishes, corruption continued unchecked. The City was untouched by the Municipal

The construction of the London Docks

Corporations Act of 1835 which reformed local government in most other corporate boroughs; and this important municipal reform did not, of course, affect the metropolitan parishes.

By 1837 the vestry system had been bewilderingly complicated by the fact that many parishes had acquired particular powers for special purposes (e.g. street paving) by private Act of Parliament; by the existence of a large number of local trusts charged with responsibility for street lighting; by the survival, north of the Thames, of more than 14 separate turnpike trusts until as late as 1826, when they were superseded by government-appointed Commissioners; by the establishment after 1834 of Boards of Guardians to administer poor relief; and by the existence of 8 metropolitan commissions of sewers. These last were not concerned with sewers in the modern sense. They were supposed to raise a sewer rate and use the proceeds to ensure the proper drainage of surface water. Frequently they performed the former function without performing the latter; and they persisted into the 1840s in the view that the protection of public health, for instance by actually enclosing the sewers, was not their responsibility. In law at any rate, there was supposed to be no discharge of household excreta into the sewers. It would thus tend to lie about in foul-smelling pools.

In only one respect, by the time of Queen Victoria's accession, did London as such possess an administrative unity: that provided by the Metropolitan Police created by Sir Robert Peel in 1829. The Metropolitan Police Commissioners were initially responsible, under the direct control of the Home Office, for an area extending 7 miles (11 km) from Charing Cross, but excluding the City itself. In 1839 the river police, established early in the century (partly out of public funds) to provide some protection against wholesale waterfront and mid-stream pilfering, were made a division of the Metropolitan Police, and the Police Commissioners' powers were extended to the whole area within a 15-mile (24-km) radius of Charing Cross. Despite the recommendations of a Royal Commission and a Select Committee that it be made part of the Metropolitan police area, the City obdurately objected and in 1840 the government was forced to content itself with an Act establishing a separate City police force under the control of the City Corporation.

The existence of the Metropolitan Police Force may be regarded as one reason (but almost certainly not the only reason) why London was relatively more orderly and good-humoured than other European capitals for the greater part of the century. After the initial resistance to them as odious agents of the central power, whose very existence was a threat to the freedom that was alleged to be every Englishman's birthright, the Metropolitan Police proved less hateful than the military; it is notable that the most ugly public disturbances took place in London in 1887 when the Guards were called in. That they were not to be submitted to coercion by soldiers was an ingrained conviction among ordinary Englishmen; and the creation of a non-military and unarmed police force rendered both riots and the provocation of riots less frequent in Victorian London than might have been the case otherwise.

It is highly significant of the state of mind of both government and people in the decade when Victoria became Queen that the one major increase in the powers of central government which then took place was in its control over the problem of law and order in London, that is to say in the physical environs of the seat of government. From 1815 until the collapse of Chartism in London in 1848, governments were in constant fear of 'the mob'. The phenomenon of large urban masses was new and disturbing; memories of the storming of the Bastille and of the Gordon Riots of 1780 were still frightening; and the note of alarm so frequent in the writings of foreign visitors to London was the normal response of men used to the fact that the populations of much smaller European capitals than London could rise up and cause thrones to topple merely by taking *en masse* to the streets.

The areas successively assigned to the Metropolitan Police were, for the whole of the Queen's reign, in excess of the area that could properly be designated London. This was because Peel and his successors wanted to give the force as large an area as possible, owing to the absence for some years afterwards of any comparable body in other parts of the country. The wholly built-up area in 1837 was to some extent bounded on the north by the Regent's Canal, but it already reached beyond it to St Johns Wood and had surrounded and almost absorbed the middle-class residential suburb of Islington. Its western edges had reached Paddington and were encroaching beyond Tyburn. In the south-west, Chelsea was not yet quite absorbed, Fulham was still a separate village, Kensington still a rural outer suburb. South of the Thames, the built-up area was about to reach the hitherto upper-class residential village of Clapham. Camberwell was already enclosed on its northern side; but there was not much continuous development south-east of Rotherhithe, though by the river were the Surrey Commercial Docks and a rather separated development in the Isle of Dogs, south of the West India Dock. North of the Thames, Stepney and Limehouse represented London's eastern limits in the 1830s. Bethnal Green and Hoxton were not yet fully absorbed and Hackney was still, precariously, a detached, if no longer fashionable, suburb. London's wholly built-up area was thus about 6 miles (10 km) across—from Tyburnia to Stepney, from St John's Wood to Rotherhithe, from Hoxton to Brompton, and, on a north-south axis, from Islington to Camberwell.

The previous two centuries had been marked by much small-scale development, principally to the east, south and south-

east of the City, much of it of undistinguished quality undertaken by small builders for small landowners. Already, well
before the Queen's reign, this area suffered from the relative
unsuitability of the low-lying and often marshy land for
building to the east of the City, and from the late accessibility
of the south-east owing to the lack of bridges. Vauxhall, Waterloo and Southwark bridges were built between 1813 and 1819,
all of them by speculators who hoped to profit from their
investment by the collection of tolls, an expectation that was
never fulfilled. It suffered also from the pull of government and
fashion exercised by the palaces of St James's and Westminster
and by the Royal Parks, to which there were no counterparts
elsewhere save at faraway Greenwich. Such small open spaces
as there were elsewhere tended to disappear under bricks and
mortar until an act of 1866 forbade further encroachment.
Victoria Park was created in Hackney by government action
in 1845, and Battersea Park in 1858; Finsbury Park was opened
in 1869 and Hampstead Heath was acquired for public access
in 1872. All these developments came too late to create new
tendencies in residential fashion, since Hampstead's reputation for healthy air and handsome views had been established
in the early eighteenth century. Hackney had been going down
the social scale ever since the beginning of the nineteenth
century and, though Battersea's development did in fact
post-date the creation of the park, it was by then somewhat too
contaminated by the mess of railway lines from which it
suffered.

The other, allied, factor was land ownership. The land
immediately south, east and north-east of the City, as well as
much immediately to the west, seems to have been mostly in
small parcels, the ownership of many of which by now seems
beyond discovery. This small-plot development had, by the
early part of the century, already surrounded the City by a
maze of streets and alleys as far west as Soho, by the close-
packed working-class and manufacturing districts of Clerkenwell, Shoreditch, Spitalfields and Stepney on the north and
east, and a narrow riverside area south of the Thames from
Westminster Bridge as far as Rotherhithe. The better-planned
areas were to the west and north-west, many developed by
builders or speculators (almost all small-scale men) who had

acquired leases from often aristocratic ground-landlords. The fourth Earl of Southampton, who owned the Bloomsbury area and the first Earl of St Albans on whose land St James's Square had been built in the seventeenth century, were among such men.

The majority of houses in the more fashionable parts of the built-up area were tall, narrow, terraced houses, many with basements. The handsome eighteenth-century squares were often planned with markets in the vicinity, and appropriate small dwelling places for those who worked in them. London's squares and the terraces were, even when intended for rich and fashionable tenants, unpretentious and unflamboyant, and the houses often backed on to noisy, squalid streets and alleys. Lord Grosvenor's great estate in Belgravia, built by one of the few great master-builders of the early nineteenth century, Thomas Cubitt*, was only in its early stages in 1837 and was a good deal more 'grand' in conception than had been usual hitherto; but Pimlico, for which he was also responsible, was less imposing.

The most ambitious endeavour, however, was the plan conceived by the Prince Regent and his architect, John Nash, for the splendid streets starting from Carlton House and St James's Palace whose general design survives (in their configuration at least) in Regent Street, Piccadilly Circus and Oxford Circus, and an opened-up Portland Place leading to the remarkable Nash-designed* terraces of Regent's Park, though fewer houses were built in the Park than Nash originally intended. Characteristically, the Nash plans included provision for a working-class market and shop area as well as for a new barracks to the east of Albany Street. The market area (Cumberland Market) survived till the 1930s as one of the most evocatively Dickensian scenes in west London. As an outlyer to the Regent Street complex, Pall Mall East was built in the 1820s to link with a new square at the top of Whitehall, which

* Cubitt also extended the Bedford estate between Bedford Square and Euston (then part of the New) Road in the 1820s.

* Only the Quadrant, the curve northwards from Piccadilly Circus was both designed and executed in detail by Nash himself. It was pulled down in the 1920s.

in 1830 was given the name Trafalgar Square. The National Gallery, built to a design by Wilkins, was completed in 1838; St Martin's Church was relieved of its encumbering poor-quality buildings and part of the north-west side of the Strand rebuilt. At the same time, to balance Regent's Park in the north, St James's Park was replanned and replanted.

The other great venture which the Victorians inherited and completed was the building of the London Docks. Until the end of the eighteenth century the City had insisted on confining direct unloading facilities to the quays on the north bank between London Bridge and the Tower. This meant a confusion of ships loading and unloading at moorings in the Port of London, with consequent delays and large-scale pilfering. In 1799, the West India Dock was authorised by Act of Parliament and was opened by 1802; it was followed quickly by the London Docks, the Surrey Docks and the East India Dock, with St Katherine's following in 1830 and the Victoria Dock in 1855. For the first time, the world's greatest port had docks that were worthy of it and they were, in the earlier Victorian period, one of the acknowledged London sights.

Generally speaking, London lacked both private or public buildings of magnificence. The aristocracy had functioned in London chiefly as ground landlords and few had constructed for themselves palaces to match the splendour of so many of the country houses which were their real homes. Devonshire House in Park Lane, Burlington House and Chesterfield House, both in Mayfair north of Piccadilly, were by such aristocratic standards relatively modest 'palaces'; they were outshone by the building now known as Lancaster House, erected in the 1820s for the Duke of York. To the same period belong the less impressive Apsley House, rebuilt near Hyde Park Corner for the Duke of Wellington, and Clarence House in St James's, built for William IV while he was still Duke of Clarence.

One remarkable feature of the West End scene—the nineteenth century London clubs—was already well established. Their older forerunners, Boodles', Brooks's and White's had retained something of the character of enlarged coffee houses. Nineteenth-century clubs were meant to impress. The United Service Club was handsomely housed at the junction of

The Reform Club, designed by Barry and opened in 1841

Lower Regent Street and Charles Street (now Charles II Street) from 1815 until it moved in 1827 to a new Nash building at the corner of Pall Mall, its original building then becoming the home of the Junior United Service Club. There followed the University Club at the bottom of the Haymarket, Crockford's and the Athenaeum, the last being built opposite the United Service in Pall Mall. The Travellers' Club was built in Italianate style by Charles Barry and in 1837 the same architect began to build the Reform Club. The size and spaciousness of these premises were a reflection of male dominance and of the nomadic existence of the leaders of the nation's life, as well as their exclusiveness. For most of their privileged habitués, 'home' was in rural England; while for an increasing number the habit of communal living in all-male communities at boarding schools established a pattern of social behaviour from which domesticity could not entirely liberate them. An absence of adequately speedy forms of private transport also kept them in London for longer periods than would be necessary a century and a half later.

Among other notable buildings of the immediate pre-Victorian period were the Bank of England, completed in 1833, a new building for the Post Office at St Martin-le-Grand, and the present British Museum, constructed between 1823 and 1847. The Victorians also inherited a number of large general hospitals from their recent past: Westminster, Guy's and St George's hospitals were already a hundred years old when Victoria came to the throne; Moorfield's Eye Hospital dated from 1804; the Charing Cross from 1818; University and King's College Hospitals dated from 1833 and 1839 respectively. The Victorians themselves were to build a large number of specialist hospitals.

London in general was relatively well supplied with a number of over-large churches. There had been a short-lived burst of church-building after 1710 but a dearth of it after 1760 just as the population began rapidly to expand. Accordingly, in 1818, an Act was passed through parliament, at the urgent desire of a Church alarmed at the spread of the new Nonconformity, authorising the expenditure of a million pounds (by the Church) on new building. The early eighteenth-century churches included St Mary-le-Strand, St Martin-in-the-Fields, with its incongruous spire, St George's, Hanover Square and St John's, Smith Square. Paddington's St Mary's and Hackney's St John's were among the few distinguished churches built in the late eighteenth century. The parish church of St Mary-le-Bone was completed in 1818 and All Souls', Langham Place was strategically placed within the

The Albert Memorial and the Albert Hall in 1869

overall visual context of Nash's Regent Street and not finally rendered invisible by obtrusive building until the 1960s.

The Victorians were to react strongly against what they considered the dull uniformity of eighteenth-century domestic architecture, and condemned classical styles as 'pagan'. The decisive moment had in fact occurred just before Victoria's accession. The destruction of the old House of Commons by fire in 1834 led to Barry's new dramatically Gothic Parliament building and gave scope to the Gothic obsessions of Pugin, who decorated it. The Houses of Parliament and Big Ben are the first aesthetic monuments of the Victorian period and they set a fashion for medievalism from which, to the very end, the Victorians, even in London, found it hard indeed to liberate themselves.

Much else that the Victorians themselves built will be referred to in the chapters that follow. They built many, indeed too many, large houses and many, but too few, small ones. In the 1870s, in Bedford Park, just east of Turnham Green, they produced the first garden suburb. They built 13 main line railway termini, many new streets and large shops and hundreds of new churches, many of them inspired by the liturgical revival engendered by the Oxford movement, the most characteristically splendid perhaps, being All Saints', Margaret Street. Only Westminster Cathedral, begun late in the century was not in the Victorian Gothic tradition since, perforce, a new Roman Catholic basilica had to be in a style different from that which was standard for the Anglicans; hence its Romano-Byzantine design. Particular specimens of Victorian architecture which are now regarded with some awe include the former Midland Hotel, fronting St Pancras Station, erected between 1865 and 1875 by Scott, and which, whatever one may think of it, remains the most fantastic building in London; the Law Courts designed by Street and built between 1868 and 1880, Waterhouse's Prudential offices in Holborn, built in 1878–79, and the Imperial Institute in South Kensington, built at the end of the 1880s. Most characteristic of all, were the Albert Memorial in Hyde Park and the Albert Hall which faces it; the former being considered the supreme example of High Victorian taste and as 'a jewel set amidst the solemn buildings of London'.

'Victorian architecture was unrepentantly derivative': the Crown Life Assurance Office, Fleet Street, designed by T. N. Deane and built at a cost of about £17,000

Even when it was not Gothic, Victorian architecture remained derivative. Norman Shaw's much-admired New Scotland Yard building on the Embankment, built in 1889, and Whitehall Court, built at about the same time, were both imitation French chateaux, for example. The reason for the growing affection for Victorian architecture in the second half of the twentieth century is much the same as that which caused the Victorians themselves to like it. They inherited an austere and often clean-lined tradition from their immediate past and reacted against it; Londoners a century later, seeing their townscape slashed by stark motorways and dominated by high, hard-edged blocks of concrete and glass, find in the loving flamboyance of Victorian building that refreshment for otherwise deprived visual senses that the Victorians themselves found in it.

Further Reading
George Rudé, *Hanoverian London, 1714–1808,* 1971
John Summerson, *Georgian London,* revised edn., 1969
M. Dorothy George, *London Life in the Eighteenth Century,* 1965
John Summerson, *John Nash, Architect to King George IV,* second edn., 1949
J. F. C. Harrison, *The Early Victorians, 1832–51,* 1971
Geoffrey Best, *Mid-Victorian Britain, 1851–75,* 1971
Francis Sheppard, *London, 1808–70: The Infernal Wen,* 1971

II

The Metropolis
and its Problems

The 115 square miles which were held to comprise the London area in the 1830s and 1840s were not in general much more unhealthy than the other large towns of the period. But this was not to say much; and the multiplicity of local authorities was so great that that pioneer of public health, Edwin Chadwick, wished to replace them all by one Metropolitan Commission with, in particular, sole responsibility for sanitary affairs. Chadwick, the most assiduous of the Poor Law Commissioners who had supervised the Boards of Guardians established in 1834, was, however, thoroughly detested. He interpreted his position as entitling him to demand that the government override the local authorities and, in the contemporary phrase 'bully the people into health'. Realising that disease was a major cause of much of the poverty with which Poor Law Guardians had to deal, he published in 1842 a Report on the Sanitary Condition of the Labouring Population whose horrifying revelations made it a best-seller. In particular, he insisted that cholera, which had caused over 16,000 deaths in England and Wales in 1832, was a direct consequence of lack of drainage, of inadequate water supply and of poor ventilation.

His advocacy of sanitary improvement was so forceful that a Royal Commission on the Health of Towns was set up in 1843. Its Report included a fierce attack on the ineffectiveness of the 7 London Sewers Commissions and the City's own Commissioner of Sewers. When, as a result of the Report, the time came to introduce what became the Public Health Act of 1848, the City was so alarmed by the influence of Chadwick and his supporters that it felt forced to act in its own defence. It quickly put up a Bill to equip the City of London with its own sanitary powers in order that the Public Health Act, with its emphasis on central control over local authorities, should not apply to the square mile. In the end, if only because the Prime Minister himself, Lord John Russell, was one of the City of London's two MPs, the City Sewers Act of 1848 left the powers of the City's Sewers Commission untouched. The only change in the metropolitan area was that a new Metropolitan Sanitary Commission of 23 members replaced the 7 former Sewers Commissions which had had a nominal membership between them of a thousand persons.

Still determined to keep its enemies at bay, the City astutely took the forward-looking step of appointing a Medical Officer of Health. Thus, surprisingly, the most antiquated corporation in the land was the first in the country after Liverpool to have its own Medical Officer. Even more surprising were the long-term effects, for the public health of the country as a whole, of the City's choice. They appointed John (later Sir John) Simon, a young surgeon on the staff of St Thomas's Hospital, already well-known as the first lecturer in pathology ever appointed to a teaching hospital. Simon's impact as MOH in the City from 1848 to 1855 was so great that he became a national figure, and was the government's own Chief Medical Officer until the 1870s, contributing enormously to all subsequent public health legislation. Appointed partly to fend off government interference and partly because of the imminence, in 1848, of another cholera epidemic, Simon proved outstandingly successful. With remarkable tenacity and above all by his annual reports, which were notable for their terseness and clarity, Simon improved the sanitation of the City and the health of its citizens, and secured widespread professional and newspaper support for the cause of public health at a time when Chadwick, for all his pioneering zeal, was fast becoming universally disliked for his autocratic methods and his contempt for the medical profession.

Cholera was only one of the principal dangers to the life of Londoners which resulted from the primitive water supply and sewerage system which characterised the metropolitan areas no less than the newer towns of early Victorian England. The particular difficulty about cholera was that nobody then knew more about its transmission than that it was associated with the accumulation of filth. That disease could be transmitted by bacilli was not known as yet and even when discovered the theory was only slowly accepted. The theory most favoured in the 1840s was that it was transmitted by polluted air, that is to say a 'miasma' set up by any collection of foul-smelling material. It was a good enough theory to start with, since at least it got the fight against filth begun and this helped, if not to eradicate cholera, at least to keep it within bounds. Cholera began with a bacillus in the intestine of one person which was then transmitted to the intestines of others either by physical contact with excrement, or by flies transmitting it from excrement to food or—and this was the reason for its epidemic proportions—by water which had become polluted with excreta, since the cholera bacillus could survive for up to fourteen days in water. Hence the flow of sewage into the Thames could spread the disease far and wide.

The first person to advance at all confidently the view that not 'poisoned air' but polluted water carried cholera was a general practitioner in Soho, John Snow. Plotting with care the places of residence of the 500 victims of cholera of whom he had knowledge during the epidemic of 1854 he discovered that every one of them had used a particular water pump in Broad (now Broadwick) Street at the bottom of Poland Street. The outbreak in the area stopped as soon as Snow succeeded in getting the local Board of Guardians to put the pump out of action. Snow had advanced his theory that cholera was water-borne in a small book published in 1849, but, although he developed the theory further in 1855, his writing made little impression. To Simon, the theory lacked scientific verification; and to supporters of the sanitary idea, Snow's theory was held to be inimical to the cause of public health, since, if it were alleged that poisoned air was not the cause of cholera everybody would cease bothering about cleansing the streets of filth. It was not until the work of Pasteur in the 1860s and of Koch in the 1880s that Snow's hypotheses were verified. Chadwick and Florence Nightingale, neither of whom had a high opinion of the medical profession, remained obstinate adherents of the miasmatist theory all their lives, unlike Simon, whose mind was more scientific.

Although cholera had first raged in 1832, it had inspired little activity by local authorities. But in the first year of Victoria's reign, when London was swept by typhus, Chadwick insisted on an inquiry, arguing that the expense of giving poor relief to individuals and families brought to destitution by the disease ought to be avoided by public action to prevent the disease. Dr Southwood Smith, of the London Fever Hospital in Islington, declared that fever of one sort or another was a more or less permanent feature of the courts and alleys of Whitechapel and Bethnal Green.

It was most likely to cause death in the vicinity of uncovered sewers, stagnant ditches and the uncleared soil of privies. The normal method of disposal of the body's waste products in the poorest parts was to throw them into the streets. Another report associated the disease with the lack of sewers and drains in the metropolis, with the large number of ditches full of decaying refuse, with unemptied cesspools and privies and also with overcrowded, ill-ventilated living conditions. What added to the misery was that, while on the one hand the increasing use of water-closets in the more prosperous areas filled the cesspools to overflowing, the water supply was so erratic that it was impossible to install these modern conveniences in the courts and alleys of the poor and impossible, indeed, to provide even piped water, since the water companies supplied water only at intervals during the day or in some parts only once a day. The inhabitants of many of the worst areas shared one watercock, from which they filled their pails when there was water available, using the water so gathered over and over again until they threw it back into the street or court, sinks in such homes (especially in Whitechapel) being unknown. Neither, in such places, was there anywhere to store the intermittently supplied water.

It was with all this in mind that the Public Health and the City Sewers Acts of 1848 had been put on the statute book. The City Sewers Commissioners could have done as little under their act as many other authorities did under the Public Health Act had not John Simon contrived to overcome the

Road works in Piccadilly: sewers being laid at the south end of Old Bond Street outside the Egyptian Hall, a well-known place of entertainment

resistance of the Commissioners and the Court of Common Council by the thorough and unanswerable mass of facts with which he confronted them during the following seven years. One advantage working in his favour was that he could be seen to be proving what the City wanted to be proved, namely that an independent local authority could put its own sanitary affairs in order without the tyrannical interference of the central General Board of Health established by Chadwick, whose demand for the construction of arterial sewers and the provision of piped water into every house was held to be the sort of thing that only a despotic country like Russia could stomach.

As soon as the expected cholera epidemic reached the City Simon set about getting statistics in order to locate the centres of the disease and got the City police and inspectors of nuisances to order the removal of filth and the clearing of noisome cesspools and privies. He arranged for the water company to provide water twice a day instead of once and had the sewers regularly flushed. These efforts, however, caused the disease to become waterborne in the summer of 1849 and it spread to hitherto uncontaminated areas. Simon organised something approaching house-to-house visiting in order to detect and treat the disease. Although the epidemic ceased in October 1849, 854 people in the City had died from it and Simon's first Report to his masters, in November 1849, was so cogently and impressively worded that, for all its length, it was printed verbatim in some of the newspapers.

Outside the City, the Boards of Guardians, notably those in St Pancras, Whitechapel and Bethnal Green, virtually refused to carry out the duties imposed on them by the Public Health Act; and in the midst of a raging epidemic the General Board itself hardly had time to keep minutes of its own meetings. Even if it had attempted to put pressure on the Guardians, it would have been up against the fact that the bad drafting of the 1848 Act gave the General Board no real powers of enforcement. Worse still, though the Metropolitan Sewers' Commission was willing to begin a main drainage system for the metropolis, the opportunity was lost in a turmoil of dissension and administrative confusion. The flushing of the metropolitan sewers, like the similar action taken in the City, spread the epidemic. There were 6,500 deaths from cholera in the metropolitan area in the month of September 1849.

In 1850, Chadwick's General Board of Health issued a Report demanding that London's water should no longer be drawn from the Thames; pure and filtered water from Surrey should be used instead. There should be one unified water and drainage authority for the metropolis. At once, there was fierce resistance from the Metropolitan Commission of Sewers, from the parochial vestries and from the water companies, a hundred of whose important shareholders were members of parliament. The Metropolitan Water Act of 1852 was therefore a feeble thing, more solicitous for the water companies than for the health of the people of London. After 1855, no water was to be drawn from the Thames below Teddington and by 1857 all reservoirs were to be covered, water was to be filtered and the supply to be constant. But the provisions were so drafted as to allow the companies plenty of scope for evasion. The result was the death of many more Londoners in the cholera epidemics of 1854 and 1866; and enormous sums had to be paid in compensation to the water companies when they were finally bought out by the Metropolitan Water Board created in 1902.

The situation thus for long remained much as it had been in the year of the Great Exhibition of 1851. *Punch*, commenting on the information that the Exhibition authorities had been required 'to supply, gratis, pure water in glasses to all visitors demanding it', declared: 'whoever can produce in London a glass of water fit to drink will contribute the rarest and most universally useful article in the whole Exhibition.' Thus, by 1854, the Southwark Water Company was still drawing on unfiltered water from Battersea, 'perhaps the filthiest stuff ever drunk by a civilised community'. There were 130 deaths per 10,000 in that company's area in 1853–54 compared with 37 deaths per 10,000 in the area of the Lambeth Water Company which drew its supply from Surrey.

The comparable figures for diarrhoea showed a like disparity. It was this which provoked Sir John Simon, by that time Chief Medical Officer to the government itself, to accuse the Southwark Company of 'criminal indifference' to the lives of 'some hundreds of thousands of people'. The failure to deal with the water companies was starkly revealed by the last great cholera epidemic of 1866. Of the nearly 6,000 deaths caused by this epidemic, 4,276 were in West Ham and Stratford, which were served by the East London Water Company, which was known to have been supplying unfiltered water.

Smallpox victims, 1868, housed in a temporary building provided by the Poor Law authorities after the epidemic of 1867

Since the maximum penalty for a breach of the 1852 Act was merely £250, it was not thought worthwhile to prosecute the company. The only good that came out of this wholly unnecessary and avoidable death-toll was that it stirred parliament to pass the important Public Health Act of 1866.

Among the various deplorable features of metropolitan and particularly City life in the first part of the reign was the condition of the parish burial grounds. There were, in the 1830s, 88 of them; they had not been enlarged for centuries and 18,000 corpses were buried in them annually, so that bodies had interment so shallow as to be purely nominal, being placed on top of bodies already themselves buried not far below the surface. The stench was unbearable and heavy rains would uncover decomposing bodies. The effect during the cholera epidemic was that graveyards became, in the words of *The Times*, 'consecrated cesspools'. At St Olave's burial ground in Bermondsey, a woman reported seeing four green, putrefying heads sticking up out of the soil. It was not until late in the 1850s that the old graveyards were at last closed.

A more widespread 'nuisance' was caused by the City markets, especially Smithfield, to which hundreds of thousands of cattle, sheep and pigs were driven through the crowded streets to be penned up for sale, thereafter being taken off to the 150 adjacent slaughterhouses. Many of these were in cellars and, in the 1840s, entirely unregulated; the refuse and blood from these places were simply thrown into the streets. Aldgate High Street was particularly fouled in this manner. Cattle not done to death in these slaughterhouses were killed in other markets, as for instance Newport Market by Leicester Square, or sometimes in butchers' own backyards. It was not until 1855 that the City could be prevailed upon, principally by Simon, to move the live cattle market from Smithfield to Islington. In 1870 a new dead market was constructed by the City at Smithfield.

It was partly on sanitary grounds that, as Home Secretary, Palmerston put forward new proposals in the mid-fifties for the reform of the government of both the City and the metropolis as a whole. Yet again the City got itself excluded from the plan of reform; and the scheme to set up seven new metropolitan councils outside the City was also dropped. Instead, the

Metropolis Management Act of 1855 was applied to roughly what was later to be the sphere of government of the London County Council. It established, not 7, but 38 new local authorities. Twenty-three of these were the largest parishes, where the vestrymen were to be elected by the more prosperous rate-payers at 3-yearly intervals. The other 15 were district boards whose members were to be elected by the vestries of the parishes which were grouped under each board's jurisdiction. The 38 bodies would, together with the City, elect a Metropolitan Board of Works, whose main function would be to construct a sewerage system to eliminate the outfall of sewage into the Thames. It was to oversee the construction and maintenance of the local sewers, for which the boards and vestries continued to be responsible. The Board also had power to make street improvements and building regulations and to make bye-laws on public health.

Although the new system was less cumbrous than the old, the Metropolitan Board of Works, not being directly elected, was too remote to generate any feeling of municipal pride and had been given few powers of enforcement over the constituent bodies which elected it. Its plans had also to be submitted to the government where the cost exceeded £50,000 and needed sanction by parliament itself if it exceeded £100,000. Thus, no main drainage scheme emerged. The Board produced a scheme costing over £2,000,000. The government countered with one costing nearly £5,500,000. The Board said the government's scheme was impracticable and would cost up to £11,000,000. The bureaucratic and technical wrangling went on from 1856 to 1858. In the summer heat of 1857 and 1858 the stench from the untreated sewage in the Thames proved so unbearable to Members of Parliament themselves that at one point in June 1858 some of the most distinguished members were to be seen fleeing from one of the committee rooms, having been overcome by the 'pestilential odours'.

The situation thus seemed melodramatic enough to persuade Disraeli, then in office under Derby in a minority Conservative administration, to strike an attitude different from his normally hostile stance on matters of public health. Announcing that the Thames was 'a Stygian pool reeking with ineffable and unbearable horrors' he saw to it that the Board was empowered

The Victoria Embankment under construction in the late 1860s: the scene between Waterloo and Blackfriars Bridges

to construct whatever main drainage scheme it thought fit, gave it power to raise the money and relieved it of the necessity to secure parliamentary sanction for its schemes. Thanks to the work of the Board's chief engineer, Sir Joseph Bazalgette, a main drainage system consisting of 82 miles of sewers was almost fully in operation by 1865 and capable of dealing with 420,000,000 gallons of rainwater and sewage a day. It was a complete success and ranks as one of the major engineering feats of the century, particularly as so much of it had to be constructed beneath areas that were heavily built upon.

Other achievements of the Board included the setting up of a unified Metropolitan Fire Brigade in 1866 and a number of street improvements, including the widening of High Holborn and the extension of Commercial Road westward to Aldgate, which was achieved between 1862 and 1870. Most impressive in the mid-Victorian years was the Board's construction of the Victoria Embankment from Westminster to Blackfriars in 1864, the Albert Embankment from Westminster to Vauxhall in 1869 and the Chelsea Embankment in 1874. The government itself had embanked the stretch from Westminster along Millbank and Grosvenor Road.

During the same period the City lengthened Cannon Street, rebuilt Billingsgate market and Blackfriars Bridge, created Farringdon Road and Holborn Viaduct, as well as the dead-meat market at Smithfield, all between 1856 and 1869. Apart from creating both Victoria Park and Battersea Park, the Board and a number of voluntary bodies secured public control of Hampstead Heath, Clapham Common and Wormwood Scrubbs. The 1870s saw the construction of Northumberland Avenue, Clerkenwell Road and Theobald's Road and the 1880s saw the building of Shaftesbury Avenue and Charing Cross Road and the enlarging of Piccadilly Circus. Apart from the freeing of existing bridges from tolls, Albert Bridge and Wandsworth Bridge were built and Putney, Hammersmith and Battersea Bridges reconstructed.

Clare Market, between Lincoln's Inn and the Strand, 1876: one of the many slum quarters demolished when Kingsway was constructed after the end of the Victorian period.

The district boards and vestries set up in 1855 survived until 1899, for most of the time being laggardly in the execution of their duties, owing to the lack of effective supervision. They appointed medical officers of health but often ignored their reports and though they appointed inspectors of nuisances, they appointed as few as they dared. They made little attempt to deal with the continuing evils of overcrowding and slums. For all the amount of building that went on in Victorian London, there was little house-building for the poor, and indeed, railway building, the street improvements and the other important public building that went on, aggravated the shortage of accommodation for the poor; the building of the Law Courts alone dislodged 3,000 people. As the better-off moved away from the centre (the resident population of the City dropped from 129,000 in 1851 to 51,000 in 1881) the poor were left behind to endure dismal squalor. The Public Health Act of 1866 empowered the vestries and boards to limit the number of occupants of both lodging houses and other houses in multiple occupation. They regularly failed to do so, being not unreasonably convinced that if they reduced overcrowding in one street they would merely increase it in another.

The actual provision of new accommodation for the poor by other than private enterprise was not seriously considered, but philanthropic bodies tried to demonstrate that working-class housing could be built at a profit. Two early bodies of this sort were the Metropolitan Association for Improving the Dwellings of the Industrious Classes, and the Society for Improving the Condition of the Working Classes. The former built 3 blocks of tenements in Spitalfields and St Pancras and the latter provided dwellings in Bloomsbury and St Giles's. Both bodies showed a profit but only touched the fringe of the problem since the rents charged were within the means only of the better-paid workers. The wealthy printer, Sidney Waterlow, established the Improved Industrial Dwellings Company in 1863 and, more significantly, persuaded the City itself to construct some artisans' dwellings. Another famous philanthropist in this field was the wealthy Angela Burdett Coutts, who built Columbia Square Buildings in Bethnal Green; another was the American-born London merchant, George Peabody, who set up a trust which, by 1897, had

A damp, dismal court and alleyway in
Victorian Southwark

Corporation Buildings in Farringdon Road,
1866

housed 20,000 people in various 'Peabody Buildings'. Octavia
Hill, however, specialised in buying broken-down houses and
repairing them, while voluntary workers visited the tenants
frequently, to supervise their general behaviour. But the sum
total of all these endeavours was to re-house very few people.

The increase of London's population in the last two decades
of the reign, the increasing importance of the City as an
international capital of finance and the growing sophistication
of the West End created something of the same angry awareness
of London's social and administrative problems that had
marked the crusading years of Chadwick and Simon. The two
quite different men who bore the same surname, Booth, helped
to highlight once more the glaring contrast between rich and
poor, between the luxury of the West End, Mayfair and Belgravia and the squalor of what was only in the 1880s coming
to be called for the first time 'the East End'. General William
Booth, the founder of the Salvation Army, and Charles Booth,
who produced between 1889 and 1903 the 17-volume *Life and
Labour of the People of London*, both attacked, the one with fiery
passion and the other with the massive weapon of patiently-
accumulated facts and figures, the wilful ignorance of most
well-to-do Londoners about the poverty which surrounded
them. In the 1880s, too, London became, for the first time

since the brief unrest of 1866 at the time of the Second Reform Bill controversy and the years of Chartism in the 1840s, the scene of angry but often successful and well-publicised working-class protest.

There was much unemployment in the winter of 1885–86, and several meetings and marches of unemployed workers took place. During one of them, windows were smashed in Pall Mall by demonstrators who had been prevented from gathering in Trafalgar Square. On 13 November 1887 came 'Bloody Sunday' when, baton charges by the police failing to keep the marchers from the Square, the Guards were called out. Two civilians received fatal injuries.

These uncharacteristic events were followed by a successful strike by 700 girls employed by Bryant and May's match factory at Bow in the East End, in protest against their dangerous conditions of work. In the same year, 1889, came the even more spectacular London Dock Strike. Dockers made a sustained and skilfully organised demand for a minimum wage of 6d (2½p) an hour. Great mass meetings were held on Tower Hill and a series of orderly marches through the City took place at intervals for a fortnight. Their leaders, who were experienced trade unionists, sensibly took the police into their confidence and the absence of violence made a considerable impression. As the dockers had no union of their own (though they announced the establishment of one when their strike began) these marches were designed to attract not only public sympathy but financial assistance, since they had no money with which to sustain them through their strike. In this aim, the dockers were surprisingly successful. Money came pouring in from such sources as collections made at football matches, the proceeds of the sale of the Salvation Army's paper *War Cry* and most substantially of all from Australia. The size of the help from this last source says much about the character of Australian society and suggest that the links between 'the Mother Country' and 'the colonies' had been forged as much by proletarian emigration as by the advocacy of 'Imperialism' among business tycoons and fashionable academics and writers in the 1880s. The Lord Mayor of London and Cardinal Manning, Roman Catholic Archbishop of Westminster, worked earnestly for a settlement and the latter was largely instrumental in securing from the employers almost all that the dockers demanded.

The social conscience of late-Victorian London had a sharper edge and a broader intellectual basis than the rather scattered emotional protests of the early Victorians. Voluntary social work in the slums became something of a cult among serious-minded middle-class women; but there was now more to it than a genteel concern to salve uneasy consciences by acts of charity towards the 'deserving' poor. The foundation in 1869 of the Charity Organisation Society, to co-ordinate charitable work in London and elsewhere, added to the volume of exact knowledge about poverty through the activities of its district visitors. On the political side, a quite new note was struck by the creation in 1881, also in London, of the Social Democratic Federation. Its founder, H. M. Hyndman, sought to propagate the ideas of Karl Marx. For a time Hyndman attracted the support of William Morris, who led a London-based revolt against both the poor aesthetics and the dubious ethics of Victorian capitalism. The Fabian Society, principally the foundation of Sidney and Beatrice

Applicants for Admission to a Casual Ward. *This detail from the painting by Sir Luke Fildes is a dramatic visual appeal for sympathy for the destitute poor. The man with top hat and bundle may be a 'toff' fallen on hard times. The deserted, bereaved or, perhaps, 'fallen' mother with bowed head is supplied with an instantly recognisable Victorian attitude of much-to-be-pitied grief*

Norah Lindsey, 1883. Rescued from squalor, scrubbed clean and in the care of Dr Barnardo's home for orphans. The face recorded by the photographer contrasts with the chubby child faces depicted by Luke Fildes.

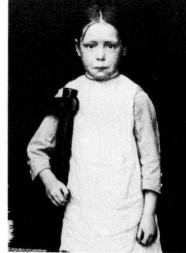

Webb, was also an essentially metropolitan organisation. There was a large output of novels and pamphlets about the social injustices of the time which reflected the renewed anxieties about themselves which the wealthy inhabitants of the capital were feeling at this time. It was a period which, whatever later historians might say, contemporaries considered a time of Great Depression. Financiers grew rich, but the wheatlands of the proudest agricultural areas of England, which had been the foundation of its aristocracy's wealth, were rapidly losing out to foreign competition; and there was a firm belief that the competitiveness of British industry was no longer what it was. As Londoners became more and more proud of their city as the cosmopolis of a vast Empire they were more and more perturbed about its failure to solve the social problems in its midst.

On the side of the workers themselves there was this new militancy among the unskilled: not only matchgirls and dockers but gasworkers at Beckton engaged in startling strikes. The ranks of the unskilled and of the unemployed ('unemployment' was a new word; that in itself reflected a growing awareness, since it was much more specific than traditional labels like 'the poor' or 'paupers') were swollen by much immigration into the capital from the corn-growing regions of the West and East Anglia. And although trade unionism had been relatively weak in much of London because of the large number of London crafts and the fact that unionism was, for unskilled workers, a luxury they could not afford before the 1890s, socialist ideas among London craftsmen considerably pre-dated Hyndman's Social Democratic Federation, and were often strong among the more than 100 working men's clubs which had existed in London ever since the collapse of Chartism in 1848.

The First International Working Men's Association had been founded in London in 1864, not merely because London was the one European capital to which political exiles could escape from the Continent, but also because they would be able to find a body of sympathisers in the metropolis. The leading figures in some of these clubs were often elderly survivors of the Chartist movement in London. The clubs were 'mutual improvement' societies or straightforward social clubs, but almost invariably their tone was radical where they were not in some sense socialist. They tended to develop towards socialism by way of secularism, being much influenced in this tendency by the reputation of Charles Bradlaugh, the MP who had refused in the 1880s to swear the usual oath on the grounds that he was an atheist. The clubs were the universities of the London artisans: they would listen to reminiscent talks about Chartism, to lectures on applied science and to poetry readings from the works of Shelley. Proceedings would be enlivened by recitations and by songs sung to piano or concertina accompaniment. Their official or ceremonial song would be

A Sunday evening meeting of 'Republican' workmen at a club in Kirby Street, Clerkenwell, 1872

Dockers being engaged for work at the West India Docks, 1886

La Marseillaise.

The more socialistic of the working men's clubs of the metropolis, as early as the 1870s, included the Stratford Dialectical and Radical Club, the Labour Emancipation League, the Rose Street Club near Soho Square, the Marylebone Central Democratic Association and, in particular, the Manhood Suffrage League. This had been created in 1875 out of a club started under the leadership of an elderly ex-Chartist called William Morgan, at the Bull's Head Tavern in Court Street, which ran south from St Giles's to Old Compton Street not far from the line of the eventual Charing Cross Road. Morgan was an out-of-work shoemaker; he was denied employment because of his activities as president of the Amalgamated Shoemakers' Society. Without clubs like these and men such as Morgan, the Social Democratic Federation would have had little working-class support and these clubs must be regarded as contributing much to the eventual creation of the Labour party and as an important factor in any balanced assessment of working-class life in Victorian London.

The first Independent Labour MP to be elected was Keir Hardie, and his constituency was West Ham South; and the foundation of the modern Labour party was the result of a meeting held in Faringdon Street in London in 1900. Thus, whereas the spearhead of working-class resistance to the established order had tended in early Victorian times to be the factory workers of the new industrial towns, the London working class contributed a great deal more to the stirrings from below that marked the last decades of the reign. The vitality of London's working class was now, much more than at the beginning, stimulated by immigrants. There were more Jews in London than in Palestine, more Scotsmen than in Aberdeen, more Irishmen than there were in Dublin and more Catholics than there were in Rome. In the central parts of the metropolitan area in Victorian times, the 'workers' were probably already 'international' before they became 'socialist'.

Meanwhile, the general ferment of ideas, moderate though it was in relation to the size of the population and the scope of its problems, caused the government of the metropolis once more to become a subject of long-drawn-out controversy. The outcome was that London's government was changed by the

County Councils Act of 1888. This transferred the administrative powers of justices of the peace sitting in quarter sessions to elected county councils. As far as London was concerned, the Metropolitan Board of Works was replaced by the London County Council, with councillors elected by ratepayers.

The coincidence of the boundaries of the new LCC with those of the old Board Works meant that it was responsible for a far smaller area than the real 'London' and did not include the City, which still continued as before to enjoy its ancient system undisturbed. All the same, the LCC was a vigorous body from the start. Lord Rosebery was the Council's first chairman and for the rest of the century the dominant influence in London government was a coalition of 'Progressive' councillors, which included such a wide range of liberal, radical and socialist opinion that it was not until Edwardian days that LCC elections began to be fought on a national party-political basis. Since, however, it was manifestly a non-Conservative coalition, this was alleged to be one of the reasons why the powers of the LCC were limited by an Act of 1899, passed by a Conservative government, which swept away the old district boards and local government parishes of London and replaced them by 28 metropolitan boroughs, each with an elected council of its own. This was thus an advance in that it ended what was antiquated, but a step back in that it obstructed the LCC's efforts to govern the metropolitan area as a single unit. The larger parishes, Kensington among them, had in fact petitioned for borough status in part out of jealousy of the LCC's powers. The new system thus tended to perpetuate the differences between the wealthy and the poorer parts of London by limiting the ability of the LCC to use the county rate for the particular benefit of the poorest parts of the metropolis.

At the end of the Victorian era, London was not only so much bigger than at the start of it; it was still, in terms of local patriotism, a place without a heart. Even when Londoners thought of their city as the heart of an empire they were never sure whether this meant Big Ben and Downing Street or Piccadilly Circus, Leicester Square and the Strand. As the local government changes of the end of the century took effect and the boroughs acquired town halls and the LCC its County

47

Hall to the south-east of Westminster Bridge, they could see that their affairs were being managed more efficiently and with less corruption than in the past; but they continued to regard their borough councils and their county council largely as invented contrivances. Worse still, there remained the absurdity that, for local government purposes, an inhabitant of Acton, Willesden, Walthamstow or anywhere east of Bethnal Green did not count as a 'Londoner' at all.

One valuable institution covering the whole of the administrative county had been created in advance of it, namely the School Board for London, the result of the Education Act of 1870. It was charged with the duty of levying an education rate to provide and maintain elementary schools to augment the pre-existing state-aided National Society and Church of England elementary schools. The London School Board was exceptionally energetic and soon built sufficient board schools to make schooling compulsory within its area. Although the schools it built were among the few examples of Victorian building in London which even the most ardent of preservationists have not been able to think kindly of, they were often the first and most impressive secular public buildings to be erected in the neighbourhoods where they were situated. They were, whatever their shortcomings in the eyes of educational experts a century later, often the roomiest, best-ventilated and most hygienic surroundings in which poor children might spend their lives at any time in the Victorian era. Almost always, the least remarkable of London's board schools were, because of the Board's greater financial resources, better buildings than those of the voluntary school societies and they attracted schoolteachers of high calibre. The work of the school attendance officers appointed to enforce the law provided a valuable addition to the growing volume of evidence about the home conditions of the poor in late Victorian London.

By the end of the reign, however, only a small proportion of children stayed in the elementary schools much after they were eleven, and the numbers receiving anything more than this basic elementary schooling were smaller still. These deficiencies were due rather to the state of the law than to any failure on the part of the London School Board. Like other progressive school boards it was much hampered by the law's insistence that the education rate should be used to provide a strictly elementary education only.

Thus, technical education in London was pioneered by voluntary effort, most notably through the muscular Christian zeal of an Old Etonian, Quintin Hogg who, in 1882, purchased the disused premises at 309 Regent Street of the Royal Polytechnic Institution. This had displayed various technical and scientific novelties for the entertainment and edification of the London public. Owing to Hogg's great expenditure of time and money and his deeply-held, if always amiable, evangelical beliefs, the Regent Street Polytechnic provided not only evening classes in a large number of technical subjects but also all the sporting, social and religious activities of a Young Men's Christian Association. The success of his endeavours led to the establishment of similar institutions in London, also called Polytechnics or Polytechnic Institutes, such as the Woolwich Polytechnic and the Borough Polytechnic.

This strange hybrid labelled 'Polytechnic' was defined in a London County Council report of 1892 as 'an institute carrying out the double purpose of providing evening recreation and education for persons of both sexes engaged in industry during the day'. The success of the Polytechnics testified to the great demand for technical education in the capital and this led to their securing financial assistance from outside sources. By the City of London Parochial Charities Act of 1883, the surplus funds held by the various charities in the 107 parishes of London were made available to help maintain and establish Polytechnics; the first grants from public funds came as a result of the Technical Instruction Act of 1889, which empowered the LCC (as it did other county councils) to give financial support to Polytechnics and technical schools. In the last part of the twentieth century, the word 'Polytechnic' has come to be applied to what are, in effect, technological universities; but the Regent Street Polytechnic (now enlarged and transformed as the Polytechnic of Central London) was the only begetter of all of them.

An even more significant contribution to higher education in the capital itself, in the United Kingdom as a whole, and indeed to a great part of the territories of the old empire was made by Victorian London. In 1828, University College had been opened in Gower Street as 'the University of London', the first successful university foundation in England since the Middle Ages. King's College had been opened in the Strand, in Somerset House, in 1831, as an Anglican answer to what was known, because of the rationalist or dissenting outlook of its founders, notably Jeremy Bentham, Lord Brougham and James Mill, as 'that godless Institution in Gower Street'. In 1836, changes were made whose effect was to make both University College and King's College constituent colleges within the University of London, while making the University itself not a teaching, but an examining and degree-conferring body. The degrees of the university were, however, open to all (including women) and so its examinations were to enable students attending, for example, Owen's College, Manchester and Mason University College, Birmingham, to obtain London degrees until the time came for these and other institutions elsewhere to become universities in their own right. In making access to its degree examinations so unrestricted, London University served more than a metropolitan need, and was indeed on the way to establishing itself as an imperial university. The major limitation placed on its effectiveness was the low standard of secondary education throughout the Victorian period, and the absence of effective state aid in this particular sphere until after the Victorian age was over.

Further Reading
F. Sheppard, *London 1808–1870: The Infernal Wen,* 1971
Royston Lambert, *Sir John Simon, 1816–1904, and English Social Administration,* 1963
Selections from *London Labour and the London Poor,* Henry Mayhew, made by Peter Quennell, 1949 and 1950
E. P. Thompson and Eilen Yeo, *The Unknown Mayhew,* 1971
Charles Booth's London, ed. A. Fried and R. Elman, 1969 (selections from Booth's *Life and Labour of the People in London,* seventeen volumes, 1889–1903)
Asa Briggs, *Victorian Cities,* 1963 (chapter 8)
Stan Shipley, *Club Life and Socialism in Mid-Victorian London,* 1971
Ethel M. Hogg, *Quintin Hogg,* second edn., 1904
H. J. Dyos, *London 1870–1914: the World Metropolis,* announced but not published when this present work was written.

III

By Road, River and Rail

Although railway construction was the greatest and most momentous activity of early Victorian England its contribution to easing the never-solved problem of how Londoners could move speedily from one part of the capital to another was slight until the mid-1860s. The railway map by the year 1837 shows that the system was at its most concentrated in the industrial north and midlands and that its principal effect for London was to provide trunk routes to and from the new industrial centres, to East Anglia, to the West Country and the south and south-east coasts.

Initially, the new railway system increased London's domination of the southern half of the country rather than of the kingdom as a whole. It did not breed a race of commuters for some time; and not until after the opening of the first underground line in 1863 did it do much for the problem of transport inside the capital. That people who could afford to do so had already begun to live away from their work is demonstrated by the rapid rise in population in Hackney, Kensington and Paddington from the 1830s onwards and the fall in the population of the City, which was rapidly ceasing to be a place of residence for anyone who had the means to live in less-crowded and less-insanitary surroundings elsewhere. But it was probably well into the 1890s before the majority of humble workers could afford the double expense of living some distance from their place of work and of paying for transport to and from it. All history of the spectacular changes in the system of public transport in London has to be studied against the fact that the working classes—and the humbler sort of clerks who were

London's railways, 1855. (The key applies to both maps.)

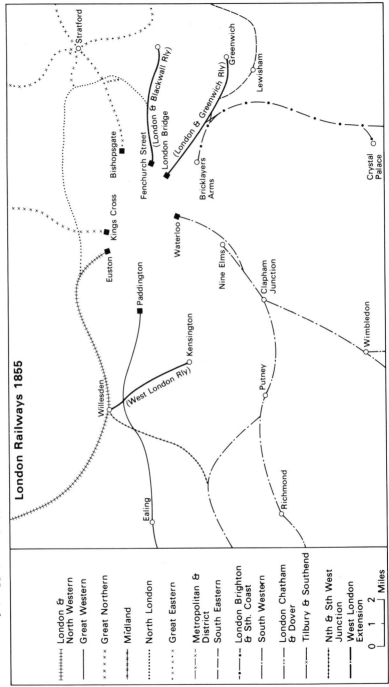

London Railways 1855

Stratford
Bishopsgate
Kings Cross
Euston
Paddington
Willesden
Ealing
Kensington
(West London Rly)
Fenchurch Street
(London & Blackwall Rly)
London Bridge
(London & Greenwich Rly)
Greenwich
Lewisham
Bricklayers Arms
Crystal Palace
Waterloo
Nine Elms
Clapham Junction
Putney
Richmond
Wimbledon

Key:

- ┼┼┼┼ London & North Western
- ───── Great Western
- × × × × Great Northern
- ┽┽┽┽ Midland
- ·········· North London
- × × × × × Great Eastern
- —×—×— Metropolitan & District
- ───── South Eastern
- —·—·— London Brighton & Sth. Coast
- —··—··— South Western
- —···—···— London Chatham & Dover
- —×—×— Tilbury & Southend
- ┼┼┼┼ Nth & Sth West Junction
- ───── West London Extension

0 1 2
Miles

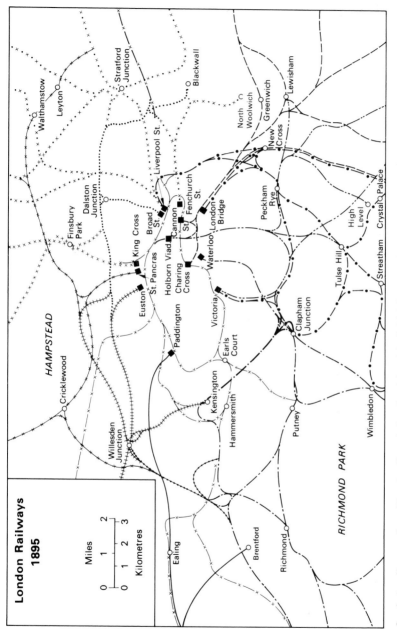

London Railways 1895

Miles
0   1   2

Kilometres
0   1   2   3

HAMPSTEAD

RICHMOND PARK

Cricklewood
Willesden Junction
Ealing
Brentford
Richmond
Hammersmith
Kensington
Earls Court
Putney
Wimbledon
Paddington
Euston
St. Pancras
King Cross
Finsbury Park
Dalston Junction
Walthamstow
Leyton
Stratford Junction
Blackwall
Liverpool St.
Broad St.
Holborn Viad.
Charing Cross
Cannon St.
Fenchurch St.
Waterloo
London Bridge
Victoria
Clapham Junction
Peckham Rye
North Woolwich
Greenwich
New Cross
Lewisham
Tulse Hill
Streatham
High Level
Crystal Palace

London's railways, 1895. (Based on Bacon's Popular Atlas of the British Isles, 1896.)

often poorer than the better-off working class—walked to their place of work, perhaps for several miles there and back. And until the 1860s, of those who did use public transport, more than 3 times as many used omnibuses and river steamers as used the railways.

For those who had no carriages of their own, the authorised conveyance was either the hackney coach seating up to 6 people or the 2-seater hackney cab. The name derived from the fact that in order to reduce congestion in the City streets, an office had been established at Hackney in the seventeenth century to limit the number of vehicles plying for hire. Only holders of hackney coach licences could pick up passengers in the paved streets of the central area of London. This system had degenerated into a typically 'corrupt' eighteenth-century monopoly. Many hackney vehicles were the dilapidated cast-off carriages of the rich and were dirty and unreliable; licences were issued to those with personal influence with the hackney coach commissioners or to persons to whom the government might wish for some reason to dispense a small measure of patronage. Hackney carriages were also expensive. Drivers charged a shilling (5p) for the trip from Westminster to Piccadilly and heaped abuse on patrons who did not add a one-third tip. Drivers also indulged in the tactic of trying to race one another through the crowded streets, partly to get to their next fare as quickly as possible and partly for the sheer excitement of it. They were a mixed lot, mostly foul-mouthed, many of them taking to the job as a last resource after dropping out of more regular employment in domestic service; others might be failed shopkeepers or clerks, or ex-gentlemen whose better days had been terminated by drink or debt.

Traffic congestion was considerable in central London, despite the new bridges, and the street widening involved in Nash's overall Regent Street plan. For most of the reign an enormous press of traffic was squeezed into the Strand and Fleet Street, the latter being particularly narrow at Temple Bar. Once Cheapside was reached, beyond St Paul's, eastbound traffic originating from Oxford Street joined that coming from Charing Cross, a problem not to be eased until Queen Victoria Street was built in 1871.

However, by 1837, not only had all tolls been abolished in

The traffic problem in Victorian London: Ludgate Circus, 1850. (From a drawing by Louis Eugène Lami.)

the central area but a start had been made on resurfacing and macadamising the principal thoroughfares. The hackney coach monopoly was terminated in 1833 by the Stage Carriages Act of 1832 and in the competition created by the new cabs victory went first to the 4-wheeled brougham, and by the 1850s to the hansom cab, one or two examples of which could still be found in the West End as late as the 1920s. As late as the 1880s the number of hackney carriages was such that their carrying capacity in the central area probably equalled that of the omnibuses, though they remained as expensive as ever and were probably used by ordinary people only when carrying luggage to or from the mainline railway stations.

For longer distances at the start of Victoria's reign, there were the short-stage coaches which, while the hackney monopoly lasted, were not allowed to pick up or set down in the paved inner area, save at their inner London terminus in the City, usually Gracechurch Street, or the West End. Outside the paved area they proceeded at a leisurely pace, stopping to pick up from their own houses passengers who had booked in advance, as well as those waiting at the regular advance booking offices, usually public houses; casual passengers might also be picked up *en route*. Such a short-stage coach could take up to 2 hours to cover the 8-mile (13-km) journey from Richmond to Hyde Park Corner, though speeds in excess of 5 miles an hour (8 kph) within the fully built up area were probably rarely attained in practice either in the nineteenth century or after. By the 1830s, London's slow-moving, jam-packed short-

55

stage coaches accounted for about one-fifth of all the stage coaches in the country. More than 50 short-stage coaches operated over 150 return journeys from the City to Paddington alone; other important routes were to Camberwell, to Blackwall (serving the West India Docks), to Clapham, Edmonton, Clapton, Hackney and Hammersmith; but one or two daily short-stage coaches went out to such rural places as Ealing, Wimbledon, Cockfosters, Cheshunt, Eltham and Bromley.

The idea of the omnibus had come from Paris since, though Paris was a smaller city, it had taller houses and therefore an even more concentrated population than London. It was as a result of the success of the first omnibuses in Paris that George Shillibeer first ran his horse-buses along the New Road, which constituted what are now Marylebone, Euston and Pentonville Roads and fulfilled in the early Victorian period the function of the twentieth century's North Circular Road. More important, the road was outside the hackney area and

The Clapham omnibus. A garden seat vehicle somewhere on what became, in the twentieth century, London Transport route 37

Shillibeer's service from Paddington Green* to the Bank was therefore free to pick up passengers and set them down anywhere *en route*. Shillibeer's venture failed, however. Starting operations in July 1829, he was bankrupt by March 1831 by which time, though he was running 12 buses along the New Road, his competitors between them were running another 78.

The future of omnibuses was nevertheless assured by the Stage Carriages Act of 1832. This not only allowed them into the central area but also reduced their tax burden, a further reduction taking place in 1839. By that time most buses carried 12 inside passengers and 3 outside; fares were at first sixpence (2½p) for short journeys and a shilling (5p) for longer. The early buses had forms on either side, straw-covered floors and conductors who, standing on a step at the back, aimed to lure,

An omnibus plying in the City near Liverpool Street station

cajole or just seize and shove as many passengers as possible onto the vehicles. There were no fixed stopping places and the buses could pick passengers up from either side of the road. Difficulties arose whenever the bus was not full, since drivers and conductors tended to hang about until they had a full complement. By 1838 conductors and drivers had to have a licence and wear the licence number on their persons so that

* His more usual starting point was in fact the Yorkshire Stingo, a public house near the subsequent site of Edgware Road tube station.

they could be reported to the authorities for offences of this nature. They could be fined up to twenty shillings (£1).

The buses, with their minimum fares of 6d (2½p), remained a middle-class preserve despite their lack of comfort and the evident inability of most early operators to keep to a proper time schedule or maintain the standards of civility which the pioneer Shillibeer had advertised as one of his principal aims. Petty clerks, smaller rentiers and minor officials, persons who, though not members of the carriage-owning class were above the status of manual workers, and who did not need to reach the City or Westminster areas before 10 a.m. and who could leave at the very early hour of 5 or 6 were the principal patrons.

Omnibus operations in London gained much from the creation in 1855 of what was originally a French-financed concern known as the *Compagnie Générale des Omnibus de Londres*. The management of its affairs was always in English hands, however, and in 1856 it anglicised its name to London General Omnibus Company, a title not extinguished till the creation of the London Passenger Transport Board in 1931. It rapidly

The Bayswater Omnibus. *This painting of 1895, by G. W. Joy, commemorates the predominantly middle-class character of the Victorian omnibus*

bought out most of the other bus companies in London, but in the 1880s had a strong competitor in the London Road Car Company which patriotically decorated its vehicles with a Union Jack. It was the London Road Car Company which introduced a proper staircase to the 'on top' of its buses, where the passengers were seated for the first time in 'garden seats' separated by a central gangway. Not until 1867 did it become compulsory for buses to draw in and pick up passengers on the left-hand side of the road only; not till the 1890s was an efficient system of ticket issue devised (by the Bell Punch Company); and the numbering of routes did not occur until Edwardian times.

In the 1890s there were about 1,700 omnibuses in London, carrying over 300 million passengers, an increase of over 200 million in 20 years. There were still over 11,000 hansoms in 1888, but their numbers dropped thereafter; this decline was attributed to the fact that City men now often used omnibuses instead or, more significantly for the future, made use of the telephone.

The other popular form of transport among early Victorians was the steamboat. The streets of inner London were clogged with largely unregulated traffic making its way through narrow streets, squelching with mud and horse dung, and frequently under a pall of grime and near-smog caused by the millions of chimneys sending forth smoke from domestic and factory fires. By contrast, the steamboats could carry hundreds of passengers considerable distances with reasonable celerity, subject to the frequency of collisions and to the inclemency of winter, though even then a frequent service was maintained. The greater part of the traffic in the 1830s and 1840s was down-river to Greenwich and Woolwich, with larger vessels serving Gravesend, Margate and Ramsgate. There was a 15-minute service to Greenwich in summer, and a thirty-minute service in winter. The fare to Woolwich was 9d or a shilling (4p or 5p), to Gravesend 1s 6d or 2s (7½p or 10p) (a season ticket for a year costing six guineas —£6.30), and for the 6-hour journey to Margate the fare varied from 8s to 9s (40p to 45p). By the 1840s small steamboats provided a regular service between London Bridge, Southwark and Westminster Bridge for 4d (1½p) and, for a similar fare, steam-

The London and Greenwich railway viaduct between Bermondsey and Deptford, in the late 1830s. Passengers are conveyed to and from the primitive station by omnibuses

boats conveyed passengers from the Nine Elms terminus of the London and Southampton Railway to Westminster Bridge. By 1850, steamboats ran a 2d (1p) service from London Bridge to Chelsea; and ½d bought a trip from London Bridge to the Adelphi. Not until the late 1850s did the railways undermine the downstream steamboats' predominance, and the underground in the 1860s ended their usefulness upstream from London Bridge.

In their heyday, the steamboats did much to establish Gravesend, Margate and Ramsgate as holiday resorts and, in the case of Gravesend, made that always resilient and adaptable town into a pleasure resort and a place of residence for persons of substance whose business required frequent if not necessarily daily visits to London. Even when the railway had begun to make the more manifest seaside pleasures of Margate, Ramsgate (and, later, Southend) equally accessible, Gravesend was still popular enough to develop a handsome promenade, a prestigious Yacht Club, a large pleasure garden at nearby Rosherville on Northfleet Reach and, within sight of Rosherville and the river, as well as on the slopes of its elevatedly healthy Windmill Hill, a number of imposing and substantial villas, many surviving, though mostly in a state of decay, a century later.

The first London railway, significantly, was built to compete with the principal steamboat route and with a particularly inconvenient omnibus route. Called the London and Greenwich railway, it opened between London Bridge and Deptford in the last year of William IV's reign, and reached Greenwich itself at the end of 1838. Its most remarkable feature, still visible and still carrying an almost insupportable volume of commuter traffic was the viaduct of 878 arches, on which its first 4 miles (6 km) of line was built. It established at once the unexpected phenomenon that railways were patronised principally by passengers and were only secondarily freight-carriers, and from this latter point of view it was an immediate success. A regular 15-minute service throughout the day at a minimum fare of 6d (2½p) brought in nearly three-quarters of a million passengers in the first 15 months of operation. Since, however, there was almost no goods traffic, the London and Greenwich did rather more than lay the foundation of what over a century later was to become the Southern Region of British Rail; it founded also that state of chronic financial difficulty from which the railways to the south-east and immediately south of London have suffered ever since.

The London and Greenwich saved itself financially by allowing its London Bridge terminus to be used by other lines: the London to Croydon in 1839, and the London and Brighton in 1841 (the two became the London Brighton and South Coast Railway in 1846), and the South Eastern (North Kent) line to Gravesend via Lewisham, Blackheath and Charlton and Woolwich in 1849. Thus the main arteries of what was to become London's most densely-used railway commuter area were already in existence by the late 1840s; by 1848, London Bridge trains also served the Kent and Sussex coasts.

The great advantage of London Bridge Station was that it was within walking distance of the City. The City Corporation was only with difficulty persuaded to allow railway penetration north of the river, but eventually allowed the London and Blackwall Railway to run into a terminus at Fenchurch Street in 1841, well inside the City and only half a mile from Gracechurch Street. The decision of a Royal Commission that no railway should be permitted south of the New Road and City Road or near Finsbury Square and west of Bishopsgate, made Fenchurch Street the innermost London terminus until Cannon Street station was built in 1866. Nevertheless, the London–Blackwall made little profit until Fenchurch Street also became the terminus of a line from the London and Birmingham

Fenchurch Street station, the one terminus allowed within walking distance of the City in the early years

Railway at Camden Town which eventually acquired the title of the North London Railway. Although it was a roundabout route to proceed from Chalk Farm to Fenchurch Street and the City by an arc through Hackney, Islington, Bow and Stepney, the popularity of this line suggests that the delays caused by congestion on the more direct road route must have been considerable, and provides evidence of how many City workers were already now living in the suburbs. In 6 months in 1851 over 85,000 people used the line to get them to Fenchurch Street. The North London steadily extended its operations out to Kew by way of Hampstead Heath, Willesden and Acton; in 1865, it acquired a City terminus of its own at Broad Street; and in 1866 constructed, at Willesden Junction, one of the busiest stations to be found on the outskirts of London, from which thereafter it was possible to run a 15-minute service to Broad Street.

The importance of this early line in the 1850s and the demand on economic grounds for its closure in the 1960s demonstrated clearly how much its early Victorian usefulness depended on the absence of the underground and tube lines at that time, and on the absence, all through the Victorian period, of the motor omnibus. For so long as it survives, the North London line (or more accurately, lines) into Broad Street provides an excellent visual introduction to a study of London change since 1850. Once so heavily used, it was by the 1960s a line almost unknown to all but the faithful few; as time went by it linked circuitously to the City, and to the City alone, decayed inner suburbs whose denizens no longer wanted to go there and more elegant outer suburbs whose work and pleasure alike required them to travel to the inner area between Marble Arch and St Paul's, to which the North London gave no access. Unlike the original London and Greenwich line it could not spread with the outward spread of the suburbs. Yet the North London was the only Victorian railway in the metropolis that returned a good dividend on its ordinary shares, and even at the end of the century it had thousands of season ticket holders and seven million journeys at special workmen's rates were made on the line every year. The population of Willesden and its environs rose from 16,000 in 1871 to nearly 115,000 thirty years later; thus well illustrating the interconnectedness of the railway and the growth of the newer suburbs.

At the beginning of the reign, the other major railways were concerned with long distance traffic. The London and Birmingham had reached Euston in 1837 and become the London and North Western Railway in 1846; but its patronage of the North London Line alone contributed to London's internal transport. The Great Western reached Paddington in 1838 but never competed for short distance traffic, though it clearly helped to account, first, for the omnibus traffic along the New Road and then to the foundation of the underground. The Great Northern, with its terminus at Kings Cross, likewise contributed little to London's transport at first; and the Midland Railway's London terminus at St Pancras was not opened until October 1868. Much earlier, the London and

St Pancras station, circa *1868, its architecture, by W. H. Barlow, contrasting sharply with the Gothic extravagance of Sir Gilbert Scott's more celebrated St Pancras Hotel built in front of it.*

Southampton railway was operational throughout its length by 1840, but had an inconveniently sited terminus at Nine Elms in Battersea; its ultimate terminus, Waterloo, was not built until 1848, being approached, like London Bridge, by a long viaduct on arches. The Eastern Counties railway (eventually the Great Eastern) slowly (and unprofitably) took in

Ipswich, Norfolk and Cambridge and had branch lines to Enfield and North Woolwich. In 1840 it had an inconvenient terminus at Shoreditch (renamed Bishopsgate in 1847) and did not reach Liverpool Street, its eventual terminus, until 1874. By the 1860s, Victoria, Charing Cross and Cannon Street stations had been built and the London Chatham and Dover Railway shared access to Victoria with the London Brighton and South Coast Railway.

The furious building projects of the 1860s provided London with a multiplicity of railway termini serving the east and south-east side of the capital and a huge tangle of lines around Clapham Junction, Brixton and New Cross. Although it is customary to dwell on the 'romance' of steam, on the technological achievement involved in all this railway building, and on the social benefits it provided, it is necessary to record how capriciously these lines emerged out of the conjunction of rival promoters' avarice with the connivance of a parliament that had the power to obstruct but could be persuaded not to, and a government that certainly regulated details but hardly ever stepped in to plan. Nor must the cost in what it became fashionable in the late twentieth century to call pollution be ignored.

One of the major reasons for the multiplicity of lines serving the east and south-east was the lower cost of buying up land in working-class districts. The building of the Docks between 1805 and 1830, the construction of Regent Street and the City's comparatively small scale street improvements in the 1830s and 1840s had all been responsible for the destruction of over 3,000 working-class houses (and therefore many more thousand household 'homes'). The railways had more devastating effects; there are no accurate figures for the early part of Victoria's reign, but the railway extensions into Charing Cross and Broad Street and the line from Shoreditch to New Cross alone displaced 16,875 people in the 1860s; the overall total of persons whose houses were destroyed between 1850 and 1900 appears to have been around 100,000. The theory was that this was a socially desirable process: the poor would leave areas of insanitary squalor and go off to live in the healthier suburbs. There was little alarm in nineteenth-century London about 'suburban sprawl' (except from old-fashioned rural radicals) for the simple reason that in the insanitary, smoke-ridden central areas the living conditions of the poor were, literally, stinkingly offensive. But the railways and omnibuses did not in the initial stages cause workers in general to live in more healthy surroundings some distance from their places of work, since very few workers could afford to pay either railway or bus fares; they moved from old slums to new ones, from fearful lodgings that had been pulled down to lodgings as bad that had not, perhaps losing their jobs as well. Displaced workers often did not move out of the district in which they had lived; they tended rather to crowd the already overcrowded dwellings that did survive railway construction. It is for this reason that property immediately adjacent to railway lines in built-up areas tended to 'go down' or, given that railways went through the cheapest sites in the first place, went still further down.

By the 1850s the increase of omnibus and cab traffic had, like all transport improvements, added to the congestion but not to the speed of traffic; yet the high cost of property in the central area precluded further surface railway development. Hence the decision to go underground, but to do so by 'cut-and-cover' railways following, as far as possible, the lines of the roads to achieve the minimum disturbance of property. In 1854, chiefly through the energies of Charles Pearson, a line was proposed to link Paddington with the London and North Western at Euston, with the new Great Northern Railway terminus at Kings Cross opened in 1852 and with the City at Faringdon Street. The first underground railway in the world, the Metropolitan, it was opened in 1863, and extended by 1865 to Moorgate, only a few minutes' walk from the Bank of England. It was dug along the lines of what are now Praed Street, Marylebone Road, Euston Road, Kings Cross Road and Faringdon Road, i.e. mostly along the length of the heavily trafficked New Road. Even this required the diversion of water, gas and sewage pipes and electric telegraph cables before the trench could be dug. Traffic had to be diverted and each section of the trench was excavated with the aid of troops of 'gravel-covered men with picks and shovels'; and the householder could see from his upper windows 'an infinite chaos of timber, shaft holes, ascending and descending chains and iron

South Eastern Railway signal box at London Bridge, 1866

buckets . . . or perhaps one morning he found workmen had been kindly shoring up his residence with huge timbers to make it safer'. In wet weather 'he can hardly get to business or home to supper without slipping and he strongly objects to a temporary way of wet planks . . . over a yawning cavern underneath the pavement'. Beyond Kings Cross the constructors had more serious problems: there was a tunnel to be driven under Clerkenwell and the sewer-enclosed Fleet River had to be crossed three times. The sewer once burst through the retaining wall, flooding the workings to up to 10 feet (3 m); but this was the only serious accident, which in an accident-prone undertaking like railway construction was something of an achievement.

At first, the Great Western and the Metropolitan worked in double-harness, so that broad gauge GWR trains could work through to Moorgate, and for a short time all the way from Faringdon to Windsor. Until St Pancras was opened, Moorgate was the first London terminus of the Midland Railway; the Great Northern also ran to Moorgate. Furthermore, connections were made with the London, Chatham and Dover, whose trains could thus run from Dover into London via Ludgate Hill. Twelve months later, in 1864, the Hammersmith and City line had extended the Metropolitan's operations, almost wholly overground, from Paddington to Hammersmith via intermediate stations at Notting Hill and Shepherds Bush.

The increased passenger traffic coming into London in the 1860s from the south, notably to Victoria and Charing Cross, created a demand for a counterpart in that area of the underground link made by the Metropolitan between the various northern main line termini. Equally desirable was an underground route to link the southern termini with the northern ones. The Metropolitan therefore built the first part of the Circle line from Paddington to Notting Hill Gate and South Kensington or, as it was then called, Brompton. Completed in 1868, this route took a long way round in deep cuttings under expensive property because of the strong objection to Kensington Gardens being dug up, which a more direct route would have entailed. This led to the circumstance that in Leinster Gardens, Bayswater, the Metropolitan had to screen the line by leaving the facades of the houses numbered 23 and 24 *in situ* so that both 'houses' are merely false fronts.

The District line extended the underground eastwards from Gloucester Road by way of Victoria, under territory even more valuably built upon than that with which the Metropolitan

The Thames below London Bridge 1870

had to contend. At the end of 1868 the District was opened as far as Westminster station, which was provided with a subway through which MPs could pass rapidly to the House of Commons. Thence, the District moved eastwards, simultaneously with the construction of a trunk sewer and the Victoria Embankment on the north side of the Thames, to Blackfriars, both the station and the Embankment being opened in 1870. In 1871, the District burrowed its way to Mansion House; but the plan to complete the Circle between there and Moorgate under the expensive territory of the City was delayed until 1884, when the Metropolitan and District lines met at last at Mark Lane station (now Tower Hill). Both railways extended eastwards to Whitechapel on the East London Railway from Shoreditch to New Cross and ran through trains from the latter to their separate Hammersmith stations.

Despite the relatively favourable accounts of the lack of excessive smell when the underground opened, complaints about fumes and smoke were being freely voiced in the 1880s, and were not greatly diminished by assurances that only rarely was the smoke thick enough to prevent the drivers seeing the signals. The general manager of the Metropolitan assured an

By this advertisement at Notting Hill Gate station the Metropolitan line pursues its 'war' against the District, 1886

incredulous public that instant relief could be found from bronchitis and asthmatic pains by resorting to the company's stations, in particular Portland Road (now Great Portland Street). As for the presence of acid gas in the tunnels, this acted, he said, as a disinfectant. Even the relatively favourable journalist from a railway magazine who, in 1893, shared the footplate of a District Circle locomotive, found the stretch west of Kings Cross so trying that he was 'coughing and spluttering like a boy with his first cigar'. However, the complete trip round the circle was made in 70 minutes, and between Faringdon Street and Kings Cross a speed of 40 mph (64 kmh) was achieved, though the speed elsewhere was between 20 and 25 mph.

Apart from these considerations, the Circle line, as a circle between Liverpool Street and other main line stations in either direction, was outdated at its inception by the introduction of cheap omnibus fares during the seventies. Accordingly, any visitor to London who wishes to recapture some of its Victorian atmosphere should, in addition to a journey on the North London, travel on a Circle train from Great Portland Street station via Aldgate to St James's Park station, observing the shallow tunnels, the frequent blow holes, the intermittent open stretches between cavernous brick walls, the enormous echoing

Charing Cross (Circle line) station, 1894

69

vaults of the stations and imagine them as being gloomier still when they were gaslit and palled with grime and smoke from the locomotives.

London was behind other cities in adopting horse trams. This was because it was already technologically ahead by the creation of the underground, and because the streets were already heavily congested. In 1869, however, 3 tramway companies received parliamentary approval, but they were not to operate in the central area. In May 1870 the Metropolitan Company began to operate from Brixton to Kennington Church and the North Metropolitan Company from White-

Metropolitan Railway steam locomotive en route for Hammersmith from Aldgate

chapel Church to Bow; on the latter route a million passengers were carried in the first 6 months of operation. At the end of the year the third company began a service from New Cross to Blackheath. The earliest horse trams carried 46 passengers and the companies agreed to charge a minimum fare of 3d (1½p) at the rate of 1d a mile; they were also compelled to operate workmen's trams at ½d a mile. Workmen's trams operated between about 4.45 a.m. and 7 a.m. and holders of workmen's tickets could return on any tram after 6 p.m. (but were required to travel 'on top only'). In fact, tram fares were soon low enough as a whole for workmen's tickets rarely to be necessary for shorter journeys. Another remarkable feature of the Tramway Act of 1869 was to give the local authorities, responsible for the streets through which the trams ran, the option to purchase the undertakings compulsorily after 21 years; and, since the tram companies were compelled to accept responsibility for the maintenance of the part of the road occupied by their tracks, they saved ratepayers money, gave them cheap transport and, as was thought at the time, provided a potential long-term capital asset.

By 1898, there were 147 miles (235 km) of tram lines in the London area, served by 1451 trams with just under 14,000 horses. Just under £4 million had been invested in the 16 undertakings then operating and in the following year the London County Council itself became a tramway operating authority and, in due course, the largest in the county area, by taking over the whole of the former London Tramway Company. Like other forms of transport, tramways were a less profitable investment for shareholders than had been expected; the fixed notion in the late-twentieth century mind that public transport showed a profit until the days of nationalisation bears little relation to the truth.

A major factor in tramway history, and one which long served to distinguish London from other great European cities, was that in 1872 parliament legislated a total ban on the entry of tramcars into central London. This deprived London forever of a co-ordinated tramway system and it was perhaps not only the low fares that were insisted on but also the statutory denial of access to the City and the West End that helped to make the tram the first form of public transport that was almost wholly of and for the working class. The trams did not, as the railways had done, add new suburbs to the built-up area in the Victorian period, if only because they were too slow-moving, but they greatly increased the mobility of the working class within it.

Significantly, in their first 5 years of operation, they operated along roads approximately in the areas first penetrated 40 years earlier by the pioneer railways: to Deptford and Greenwich; to Poplar and East India Dock, and, through Mile End and Bow, to Stratford, centre of the Great Eastern Railway's marshalling yards, repair shops and engine sheds. The role of the tram in developing growing working-class areas in and around Stratford and West Ham and in linking them with the gas, chemical and soap-making concerns in Dockland and with the docks themselves was considerable. In 1872 the railway works at Stratford employed 3,000 men (twice as many as in 1860) but by the end of the reign 6,800 were employed.

The other early tram routes in the south-east also followed traditional routes: to Brixton, Camberwell, New Cross and Clapham. In the north the trams mainly served

London's earliest electric trams at the London United Tramways' terminus at the east end of Shepherds Bush Green, 1901

heavily concentrated working- or lower middle-class areas. Kentish Town, Holloway, Highbury, Stoke Newington, Dalston and Hackney all at last had really cheap transport to the fringe of the central area of London. By the end of the century the trams were going as far out in the south-east as Woolwich and Plumstead and in the north were reaching Tottenham, Edmonton, Walthamstow and Leyton. Due west, London United trams operated from Shepherds Bush and Hammersmith to Kew and Richmond. In 1901 London United became the first London company to electrify its lines, and extended them to Uxbridge, Hounslow and Hampton Court.

In the late 1890s, with fares averaging at 1d per journey, trams carried about 280 million passengers annually compared with the 300 million covered by the omnibuses, figures which demonstrate a remarkable growth in the few years since their introduction. They were extremely slow-moving (on account of their large carrying capacity) but so frequent that they drove the omnibuses off the street in some parts of south London. Trams from Brixton and Clapham to Kennington, for example, ran at intervals ranging from every 2 minutes at peak times to every 4 or 5 minutes at other times.

Suburban railway traffic grew enormously north of the river in the last 20 years of the reign. Much of this growth was due to the introduction of workmen's tickets. These had first been issued on the Metropolitan in 1864. By the Cheap Trains Act of 1883, following complaints that there were unoccupied houses in Willesden, Hammersmith and Battersea because of the lack of cheap fares, railway companies could henceforth be compelled to issue workmen's tickets. It was also thought that this was a proper gesture of social compensation for the railways to make in view of the number of working-class people they had driven from their homes.

By the 1880s, the Great Northern's lines were heavily used by commuters moving out to Hornsey and Finchley; the latter was typical of many outer suburbs in doubling its population between 1880 and 1900. The Great Northern operated an annual total of over 25 million single suburban journeys in the 1890s, a fifth of all its passengers using workmen's tickets. A quarter of all such tickets issued in the London area were however used by travellers on the Great Eastern, which was universally known as 'the poor man's railway'. It conveyed 8,000 people a day in the mid 1880s from Ilford, Forest Gate, Edmonton and Walthamstow; and it is a measure of what working hours were like in the late Victorian period that the Great Eastern's workmen's trains all reached Liverpool Street between 5 a.m. and 6 a.m. By the late 1890s, there arrived daily at Liverpool Street 10,000 workmen's ticket users, followed thereafter by up to 35,000 clerical workers who also rated cheap fares if they arrived before 9 a.m. With 30 million single journeys daily being made into and out of the City on the Great Northern and 70 million being conveyed to and from Liverpool Street or Fenchurch Street, it is not surprising that the population of Tottenham rose from 36,574 in 1881 to 102,041 in 1901, that Hornsey's population more than trebled and Wood Green's almost quadrupled in the same two decades. If to all this there are added the North London's 34,000 season ticket holders and its 7 million workmen's ticket journeys a year, it can be seen how these railways encouraged, and coped with, a 14-fold increase in the number of people living north of the Thames outside the area bounded by Hammersmith, Hampstead, Finsbury Park and Poplar.

South of the river there was also considerable travelling by workman's ticket from as far afield as Weybridge and Dartford, for each of which the workman's return fare was 9d (4p). Threepenny workmen's returns were available to the present Southern region termini from Peckham Rye and Clapham Junction and fourpenny returns from Wandsworth, Deptford, Streatham, Norbury and Crystal Palace. Railway traffic into these termini from the suburbs was, however, by the end of the century, less than that coming in on the Great Northern, Great Eastern and North London lines. The reason for this may well lie in the fact that the tradition of regarding the river as a barrier was too deeply entrenched among the working classes to be easily broken down even by the extraordinary traffic revolution of the years after 1860. Only when to the workmen's trains were added cheap tram and cheaper bus fares at the end of the 1880s did the transport revolution begin to break down the traditional immobility of London workers. That carpenters living in Hammersmith were to be found

Workmen's trains arriving at Victoria station, 1865

working in various parts of London in the 1890s was still
considered something of a novelty. The London working class
was still markedly regional and the amount of cross-river
movement by workers was still small by the end of the reign.

The working classes south of the river had stronger links with
Kent than with workers north of the Thames, and were
markedly concentrated in the engineering, carpentering and
bricklaying trades. They tended, in their stretch of territory
from Battersea, through Lambeth to Bermondsey, Deptford
and Woolwich, to be strongly radical and nonconformist and
to have well organised trade union branches. Workers north of
the river were less well organised, and probably poorer: the
small-craft traditions of Clerkenwell and Bethnal Green with
low wages and often sweated conditions made for a lack both

of mobility and cohesion. Each small part of these areas was in many ways an urban village which population-growth had caused to be joined together physically, but in no other sense. The very poor, therefore, tended to stay where they were. Often quite respectable unskilled workers continued to live in overcrowded courts and rookeries among the criminal elements simply because this kept them within walking distance of jobs. The working classes to be found in Chelsea, Marylebone and Paddington were cut off from those to the east by the great residential and business wedge west of Regent Street and by Hampstead and Highgate.

Thus, trams and workmen's trains apart, the transport system contributed mostly to the outward spread of the considerable part of the metropolitan population that ranged socially from the lower-paid clerk and the best-paid artisan through the whole gamut of the professions and occupations up to and including those who were well enough off to have neither full-time profession nor full-time occupation.

In 1890, London acquired its first genuine 'tube' (i.e. deep-level tunnel) electric railway, operated by The City of London and Southwark Subway Company, which soon changed its name to The City and South London Railway. Operating in the first instance from a station near the Bank, it went as far as Stockwell. By the end of the Queen's reign it operated northwards to The Angel (Islington) and southwards as far as Clapham Common. It was operated by small electric locomotives pulling 3-car trains, each car seating 16 passengers on either side; at the end of each car was a platform on which rode a conductor to open the gates to let passengers in and out and to tell them where they were, since on the grounds that there was nothing to see, there were only very small slit windows. This caused the early City of London cars to be known as 'padded cells' and its heavy use at peak hours (but only then) caused *Punch* to call it 'the sardine box railway'. The second London tube, though normally referred to by its morning and evening clientèle as 'The Drain', was also something of a 'sardine box' railway. Opened in 1897, this was that vital link in London's transport system, the Waterloo and City line, running under the Thames from the main line terminus to the Bank. It operated from the start with 2-car trains consisting of a motor-car and a trailer, and the original stock was still in use as late as 1940. Never a part of London's underground railways as such, and without intermediate stations, its separateness from the main line platforms at Waterloo has always meant that it is normally used only by travellers encumbered with nothing more than a brief case, an umbrella and a newspaper.

The popularity of travelling by 'tube' was not therefore achieved until the end of the reign, with the opening, in July 1900, of the Central London line, known as 'the Tuppenny Tube' long after it had ceased its original practice of charging a flat-rate fare of 2d. Opened by the Prince of Wales, it ran from Shepherds Bush to the Bank and was an instant popular success. In the first 5 months of its life it carried 14 million passengers and provided trains from 5 a.m. till midnight. Running as it did under one of the main London traffic arteries with stations in Holland Park Avenue, the Bayswater Road, Oxford Street, New Oxford Street and Holborn, the Central served a thriving residential district, a busy West-End shopping street and also reached the heart of the City. In these circumstances it could hardly fail; it cut across the horseshoe of the Hammersmith and City Metropolitan line and was faster by far than any form of road transport, most of all in the perpetually traffic-ridden reaches east of Marble Arch. The 'tube' and its electric trains were to make the major contribution to the next phase of the never-ending revolution that London's traffic seems forever to require.

Further Reading
T. C. Barker and M. Robbins, *A History of London Transport, vol. I, The Nineteenth Century*, 1963
R. H. G. Thomas, *London's First Railway, the London and Greenwich*, 1972
J. R. Day, *The Story of London's Underground*, 1963
C. Baker, *The Metropolitan Railway*, 1951

London Transport, *100 Years of the District Railway*, 1968
M. Robbins, *The North London Railway*, 1946
C. Klapper, *The Golden Age of Tramways*, 1961
London, Aspects of Change, ed. Ruth Glass, 1964

IV

Shops and Shopping

A surprising proportion of buying and selling continued to take place in open markets in the early years of the reign, usually of course with Saturday night as the busiest time. Among the more celebrated London markets was that in the New Cut in Lambeth, where one could buy a ha'porth of sweets or Yarmouth bloaters at 3 for a penny, hot chestnuts at 20 a penny, and where butchers yelled 'buy, buy, buy, bu-u-uy' as they were still to do in those London street markets that survived into the twentieth century. Street-selling outside the markets was, at the beginning of the reign, still one reputable way in which wives of the poorest husbands could add to their income; they might buy a few odds and ends of fish, meat or fruit at the close of a market and then hawk them round. Muffins were regularly offered for sale in residential districts by itinerant muffin men. The muffin man would carry his wares on his head in a tray, covered with baize, perhaps, and accompany his cry of 'muffins for tea' by the ringing of a handbell. This traditional call could still be heard occasionally in the gathering dusk of quiet Sunday streets as late as the early 1920s; and a particularly whining version of the historic female London call, 'Won't you buy my sweet lavender' could be heard in Mayfair from time to time even during the Second World War.

Such shops as there were to supply the poorest with meat would sell tripe or other offal and bits of bacon, spiced perhaps by the coaldust drifting off the coal which might be sold there as well, together with spillings of the ale that sustained the shopkeeper in his long day's work. Near the Tower there was

Sunday morning in the New Cut, Lambeth, 1872. The policemen work in pairs

still Rag Fair, famous for its second-hand clothes shops for the
poor, as was Monmouth Street in Seven Dials; and close by
such premises were pawnshops which had to serve the poor as
an alternative to the twentieth-century hire-purchase system.
Few shops selling to the poor could survive if they insisted on
cash payment, and even payment in arrears would often be
impossible without recourse, by Thursday night, to raising
something at the pawnshop—in the hope of being able to get
it out of pawn if the week-end did not drown too much of the
husband's wages in drink. Some of the stock in the old-clothes
shops would probably have been stolen, or bought from the
pawnshop's unredeemed clothing stock. The selling of old
clothes had also been traditional to the area around Houndsditch at least since Tudor times, that is to say long before the
poorer members of the Jewish community, admitted to the
country once more since the time of Cromwell, made that trade
and that area peculiarly their own. The wearing by the poor of
the cast-off clothes of the rich, even when they had been cast

80

off a good many times before the final wearer bought them as little better than rags, was one of the features of the London scene that distressed Hippolyte Taine on his visit to England in the late 1860s.

This tatterdemalion attire, which has clad four or five bodies, I always find painful to see. It is degrading: by wearing it a person admits or declares himself to be one of the off-scourings of society. In France a peasant, artisan or labourer is a man who is different but not inferior. His working blouse or overall is his own, as my suit is my own; it has been worn by nobody but himself. This readiness to wear rags is more than mere singularity; it denotes a want of proper pride; the poor, in this country resign themselves to being other people's door-mats.

The poor were attired in this tatterdemalion dress precisely because they were neither artisans nor peasants; the women could not afford to buy made-to-measure garments, and ready-made clothing was still comparatively rare, often shoddy and at this time too expensive for the really poor. Even the better off among poor women might be glad of cast-off dresses, as for example, those passed on from their mistresses by daughters who were in domestic service, for the practical reason that the quality was good. Much female as well as male clothing was sold by virtue of its durability so that the better off were likely to 'hand on' their garments long before they were worn out and, in the case of women, merely because they had ceased to be 'the fashion', and there was always, too, the faint hope, if the dress or the coat were not too grotesquely ragged, that one could give the impression, as the phrase went, of having been 'reduced to rags' rather than of having been born in them. To wear clothes that, even in a perhaps distant past, had adorned a lady or a gentleman was in fact one stage prouder than proclaiming by a uniform that one had neither a past, nor a future hope of social betterment. Indeed, if Taine is to be believed, middle-class women of wealth had such a lamentable lack of taste and colour sense that they could look hardly less common in their current attire than the tarts who might eventually flaunt it after buying it in Rag Fair or Seven Dials.

The whole neighbourhood of Whitechapel was distinguished in particular for its markets, hawkers and costermongers. The most important in the area in Victorian times was in the Whitechapel Road, where on the broad pavement of its northern side so much was sold, from beds to boots, books to bloaters and workmen's tools to flowers and seeds that they declared in the locality you could furnish and feed a whole household and stock a garden merely from this one market.

Fish for sale by auction in Columbia Market, 1886

There was of course no restriction on hours of business and by the light of greasy oil burners or naphtha lamps, or a mere candle or two, the sellers' calls and patter could go on until midnight. In addition to the more substantial offerings, food such as jellied eels, pea soup, hot pies could be bought, or scraps of old bones to take home to turn into soup oneself if there was anything to cook them by. Then, and for as long as street markets survived, there were the vendors of quack medicines, whose leathern lungs, resourcefulness of repartee and capacity to simulate profound conviction would in a later age have got them into RADA without difficulty. Hanging around would be beggars; or near-beggars, selling fruit, toys or flowers; musicians, acrobats and strongmen, and, recurrent figures in urban and indeed suburban life for another century, Indians selling scarves. It may be asserted that, the squalor and the poverty notwithstanding, the strident, multi-coloured intensity of these street markets was something that nobody brought up in their neighbourhood would ever forget. The lusty vulgarity mingled with the pathos, the animal vitality, the swiftness of speech, the glare of the lighting, and the depth of the shadows, the cosmopolitan excess of it all and the nerve-tingling sense that every successive step would bring one face to face with the totally unexpected; out of all this came the spirit that made the music hall and made Londoners, especially those within earshot of the Elephant and Castle or the White-chapel Road, a people apart from suburbanites and provincials.

Nevertheless, there was for some time fierce competition between the older Jewish street traders and the newer Irish invaders coming in the aftermath of the Great Famine of the late 1840s. The Irish in fact displaced many Jews from the fruit business and many English from their costermongering. It was partly, thought Mayhew, that the tough, country-bred Irish lad could live harder, go without boots and stockings and do without the local Jewish amusements of draughts, dominoes or penny concerts in the evenings; altogether less civilised and un-urbanised, coming so recently from a land where, with the potatoes all blackened, a turnip to munch was something to be thankful for, he was well able to undercut the Jews. When the unrest and persecution in Eastern and Central Europe between 1848 and 1850 (and again in Poland in 1863) produced a further influx of Jews it was only by keeping rigidly within clearly defined communal boundaries that Irishmen and Jews could survive in peace in those parts. In Rosemary Lane market (now Royal Mint Street by the Tower) the Irish were particularly strong, their women's fecklessness as housewives being redeemed only by their persuasive garrulity as street sellers. Nevertheless, Rosemary Lane's Rag Fair had been a place of ill-repute for well over a century before the Queen began her reign or her famine-stricken Irish subjects came to sell there. The Irishmen found jobs as navvies when railway building was at its peak (the dependence of England's transport system on immigrant labour is as old as the system itself) or casual work as dockers and bricklayers' mates. Failing that, they joined their women as street sellers. The women were not necessarily very energetic at their selling. Country folk from a foreign land untouched by the urban revolution and unaccustomed to the pent-up life of warren-like alleys and courts, they might merely sit on the pavement or lean against the wall outside their 'homes' with perhaps baskets of dried fish for sale, in a state of stunned apathy.

Greenwich milkman, 1885

For reasons which are not altogether clear, though in 1851 at least 5 per cent of the London population was of Irish origin, the renewal of Jewish immigration in the last quarter of the century made the Irish in London far less noticeable; perhaps because many of them emigrated to the United States while others, as time passed, emerged into more stable jobs while nevertheless retaining their Irishness on account of their Catholicism, which in itself set them apart from the narrowly Protestant attitude of both the religious and the indifferent. The Jews made the area around Petticoat Lane peculiarly their own in the second half of the Queen's reign. Quite apart from old clothes selling, the Jews of this area might be glaziers, fruiterers, tailors, shoemakers or picture-frame makers; they might deal in old clothes from a Houndsditch shop and a Petticoat Lane stall.

Strangely, whereas Mayhew, writing in 1859, found some Irish homes clean and tidy, writers on Jewish homes in Whitechapel later in the century found many of the poorer ones squalid. The English and Irish seem to have been readier as they prospered to spend their extra cash on the home, the Jews preferring to spend it on food, smarter clothing and on theatres and concerts, perhaps a reflection of their longer tradition of city life and perhaps, too, their greater intellectual vivacity and their aloofness from the tendency of both Anglo-Saxon and Irish to regard a relentless consumption of beer or spirits as a major form of 'recreation'.

By the end of the century, some of the more successful East End Jewish families had migrated to parts of Kensington; the northern part of that borough certainly had a large Jewish element at various income levels, so that there were complaints that the better parts of North Kensington were 'going down' on account of them. Those who remained to trade in the East End lived in a gregarious huggermugger quite removed from the English tendency to segregate themselves off into one-family units as soon as they could afford to.

As late as the 1880s and 1890s, Charles Booth's survey of *London Life and Labour* found plenty of scope for his zeal for classification (and chilling disapproval) among the members of the East End's street market community. The poorest were the organ grinders, acrobats, professional beggars and those near-beggars who sold penny oddments from trays slung round their necks. Buyers of old clothes and boots for renovation, and scrap iron dealers were other groups in the lowest ranks of the poor.

'Wild rabbits!'

A 'hokey-pokey man':
Italian ice-cream vendor,
1877

There were also, slightly better off, casually employed musicians, chair caners, street glaziers and, better off still, 'public musicians with regular work, billiard markers, scene painters, travelling photographers, costermongers with capital in stock and barrow and perhaps a donkey, coffee stall keepers, cats'-meat men and successful general dealers'. In Booth's time Petticoat Lane (Middlesex Street) had become the general market for the Whitechapel area. He distinguishes between general dealers who were 'small itinerant merchants' and street sellers, who stayed put, offering their stock from 'a stall, a barrow or a basket'.

Most general dealers were Jews and some of them, he said 'buy and sell in a large way and handle large sums of money'. Nevertheless their way of life (as has been suggested earlier) did not differ greatly from that of other poor Jews; and Booth hinted rather darkly that only the police really knew just how they acquired either their stock or their wealth. He clearly preferred street sellers on the grounds that they were 'open and palpable servants of the public' but he disliked the discovery that 'costermongers of the upper grade are a very well to do lot', and that successful street traders, though of a 'much lower social grade and in fact a rough lot', were better off than many skilled workmen. He noted that casual and unskilled workers continued to take to street trading in slack times and to do rather badly at it. Booth viewed Petticoat Lane with characteristic middle-class disapproval as a place where 'trash' was sold— cheap garments, smart braces, sham jewellery, old clothes and boots, chipped china shepherdesses 'and rubbish indescribable', fish, vegetables, fruit, 'queer cakes and outlandish bread'. Nearly always, the account goes on, 'the Jew is the seller and the Gentile the buyer; Petticoat Lane is the exchange of the Jew, but the lounge for the Christian'. Booth also noted, near Shoreditch station, the street markets devoted to the sale of birds, cats, dogs and other pets (surviving in Club Row on twentieth-century Sundays, as does the Petticoat Lane market). Booth also reported the survival in the last decade of the century of street markets 'in every poor quarter of London'.

Others that long retained their Victorian flavour were to be found, for example, in Berwick Street in Soho, hard by the starting point of the London cholera epidemic of 1854; in the Portobello Road in North Kensington (long before it was 'discovered' by the *chic*); and in Shepherds Bush, originally under the railway arches between Uxbridge and Goldhawk Roads, but spreading to include stalls on the roadway, and referred to, therefore, by locals, as '*down* the arches'. Characteristic of them all were 'the flaring lights, the piles of cheap comestibles and the urgent cries of the sellers'. In Booth's mind these cries were accepted on both sides 'as necessary though entirely useless', an obtuse observation which brands him (or was it rather his young assistant researcher, Mrs Beatrice Webb, née Potter) as without understanding of the basic requirement of a form of salesmanship that had perforce to be vocal, and the psychology of potential purchasers, who had not heard of the phrase *caveat emptor* but were bound to act upon its principles by the leanness of their purse and by the knowledge that, if they played dumb long enough, the sellers of many goods would bring their prices escalating down to something more like what a canny customer was prepared to pay.

The more English costermongers outside the East End may not have been as suspiciously well-off as Booth claimed to find some of those in the Whitechapel area. Certainly, those who were mobile rather than static tended to be in perpetual trouble with the police if only because the latter regarded costermongers as one of the few contributors to traffic congestion whom they could easily charge with obstruction. They were forever being 'moved on'; and the coster who was slow to obey this instruction was liable to have his stock and his barrow impounded. Moreover, costermongers tended to become, as the reign proceeded, over-committed to the poorest of the poor; people who could afford to use shops soon did so once there came to be a sufficiency of reliable ones. In the middle years of the century 1 cabbage out of every 3 sold in London, and half the apples and pears were sold by costermongers, and they handled a high proportion of the cheaper sorts of fish, chiefly herrings, winkles and (in those days) oysters. But selling low-priced fruit, vegetables and fish to the very poor under constant police surveillance, and in the face of hostile, ratepaying shop-keepers, was a precarious way of making a living, particularly since the costermonger was at the mercy of the weather; a few days' rain would deprive him of customers and a sudden heatwave could make his wares stinking and rotten. Many costers did not own their barrows, but hired them at exorbitant rates. To survive at all required adroitness, toughness and a quick eye for the main chance, and compelled a way of life that, because it was treated by the police as quasi-criminal, could easily become so in fact. Hence their close-knit sense of community, with its tendency to develop the special language of back slang (such as 'esclop' for 'police', which in time became 'slop') or rhyming slang (such as 'apples and pears' for 'stairs'). This was less of a secret code than the parallel habit of public schoolboys and undergraduates of expressing their corporate spirit by using an equally tribal kind of private jargon.

The costermonger image created by the music hall stars such as Albert Chevalier and such music hall songs as *Knocked 'Im in the Old Kent Road* emerged only when the reality was ceasing

Respectable Soho bookshop in Dean Street.

Artistical sign-writing tobacconist's shop in Clerkenwell, 1841. The posters advertise steamboat trips to Margate, 'concerts d'hiver', a play (High Life Below Stairs) *and the Royal Polytechnic Institution*

to be more than a survival. And although the flash coster-monger had often worn jackets with pearl buttons, the pearly costume donned in later years for special occasions, and even more the ostrich feather hats of the costers' women, bore as little relation to the realities of Victorian costermongering in general as the ceremonial attire of Life Guards did to, say, the realities of the Boer War or the 1914–18 War.

It was understandably a long time before the Industrial Revolution produced a shopping revolution to reflect it; something like a century, in fact. For most of Victoria's reign, the typical shop was a small, independent one-man establishment. Butchers bought their meat direct from the live market at Smithfield and there were still as many as 700 cow-keeping establishments in the London area as late as the 1880s, indicating how long it was before the effects of large scale milk conveyance by rail from country to London were fully felt. Although shopkeepers were considered as extraordinarily low in the social scale, they had in general to be skilful at buying stock, since nothing was standardised. The grocer himself chose and blended the tea he sold and had to weigh and package it himself. The haberdasher, without benefit of cotton reels,

89

bought cotton and thread by weight and disentangled it into suitable lengths himself. Only the most successful of shop-keepers graduated from retail selling to selling to lesser shop-keepers in quantity at a discount, and from thence to the hitherto almost unknown category of wholesaler.

True, shops brightened up in the early nineteenth century, with the coming of plate glass and, soon afterwards gaslighting, but drapery, as the retailing business that owed most to early industrial change, was the only one to show much initiative. Drapery included dress materials, general household drapery and also hosiery, gloves and general haberdashery. Since such goods were the first to show signs of mass-production for a cheap market, there emerged the type of draper who relied on low profits but quick returns; who pushed handbills through letter boxes, and who, to ensure a rapid turnover, would cut the prices of items that were not selling fast enough, or an-nounce a sale at specially reduced prices of 'slightly defective' stock, salvaged, he said, from a fire in some other shop. Such shops also appear to have been the first, in the early years of Victoria's reign, to make use of price tickets. This was immediately hailed as the sign of a shop to be avoided by the genteel. It was hardly decent to demand the immediate cash payment of a sum on which there was to be no reduction and which was advertised to every common passer-by. A century later, the attitude was reversed: a shop which did not display price tickets might well be avoided on the grounds that it was bound to be prohibitively expensive. By the 1850s, however, fixed prices in London were the general rule, though the price ticket did not become general in good-class shops until the advent of the departmental stores.

Just as steam-powered textile mills had meant child and female labour and long hours, so at the far retail end of the economic chain, larger gaslit drapers' shops (and gaslit streets, making it easier to shop late at night) meant more underpaid shop assistants working very long hours, and living over the shop in conditions that made both early rising and late bedding-down easier and perhaps a welcome exchange of one dis-comfort for another. Such assistants rose at 6 a.m. and found their working day ending at perhaps 10 p.m., with midnight not unusual on Saturdays. And the long working hours that prevailed among all classes could mean Sunday opening as well as all-day trading on Saturday, since so few workers could get to the shops on any other day. Half of London's shops opened after 10 a.m. on Sundays in the 1840s.

Although the middle-class (and aristocratic) reformers of the capital were successively provoked to display moral disapprobation of negro slavery or child and female labour in factory and mine and were increasingly outraged by 'the condition of the poor' they were slow to campaign on behalf of exploited shop assistants, since shop assistants tended to be taken for granted and treated almost as domestic servants. They would be hardly readier to support shorter working hours for shop assistants than for parlour maids or pantry boys. Yet, as shopkeepers of the more humane sort insisted, reform could only come by government legislation; for a shopkeeper to decide on his own initiative to reduce assistants' hours meant, almost certainly, closing earlier than his competitors and therefore loss of business. The Metropolitan Drapers' Association themselves took the lead in campaigning against long hours in 1842, and in 1847 renamed themselves the Early Closing Association; but while larger establishments, notably Debenham's and Marshall and Snelgrove, were prepared to co-operate, the smaller ones were not. In the main, the rich went home to dine at about 6 or 7 in the evening and no lady would be out and about the streets after that hour; for the poor, however, this time of the evening was probably the first opportunity of the day to do any shopping; and brightly-lit, well-stocked shops of a night-time were, like the street markets, perhaps the one bit of colour in their drab lives.

In 1871, Bank Holidays were established; but when the originator of the Bank Holiday Act, Sir John Lubbock, tried to get a ten-hour day for young shop assistants through parliament in 1873 he had no success. Not till 1886 were young persons (i.e. those under 18) forbidden to work more than 74 hours a week. Adult shop assistants had no legislation in their favour in the Victorian period, and continued to work an average of 80 hours a week. The Oxford Street store of Marshall and Snelgrove was unusual in allowing its assistants a 40-minute lunch break and a 20-minute break for tea. Normally, an assistant could expect no more than half an hour a day for rest and refreshment, and was on his or her feet virtually the whole time. Even where seats were provided, assistants might be fined or dismissed for using them. Shopkeepers believed that shoppers would consider the place ill-patronised if they found assistants sitting down. The lack of fresh air added to the discomfort of the job and so did the fact that the moment a young female assistant was indiscreet enough to marry she was instantly dismissed. Even if she avoided the snares of matrimony, the woman shop assistant, by the time she was 40, was liable to consumption and varicose veins and to be unfit for further employment. A shop assistant might earn between £25 and £40 a year apart from food and lodging, such as they were. Sometimes he would also get commission on sales and thus become a pest, pushing timid customers into buying more, or more expensive, goods than they intended. In the absence of a system of commission, assistants could prove lethargically indifferent.

The general trend of shopkeeping in the nineteenth century was to move westward. For obvious reasons, there were few important shops east of the City and fewer within it than there had been. There were two large drapery establishments in Shoreditch: John Hopkins, specialising in linen, wool and

Shoreditch High Street, 1896: street traders on the left and, in the background on the right, Rotherham's long-established drapery warehouse

silk (bought by customers in lengths for making up into dresses by themselves or by a dressmaker) and Rotherham's, who were already wholesale drapers. The name of Spink, in Gracechurch Street, had been associated with gold, jewellery and sporting guns for nearly a century. Near London Wall was the Fore Street Warehouse, a long-lasting retail and wholesale drapery concern. By St Paul's Churchyard there was an abundance of well-established shops, though their claim to pre-eminence could perhaps be challenged by those of Ludgate Hill. On a corner north-west of St Paul's there were the handsome premises of George Hitchcock & Sons, distinguished by Greek columns, the largest plate glass windows in London and the pioneering of gaslight for the lighting of window displays. Silks, velvets, laces and ribbons, Chinese shawls and carpets were there in abundance. On Ludgate Hill, a City Alderman, Robert Waithman, had an outstanding display of shawls from India and the Far East as well as damasks and muslins. Waithman became a member of parliament; but his speeches, being those of a shopkeeper, were liable to be punctuated by throaty noises of disapproval from his fellow-members.

Further west, near the diamond merchants of Hatton Garden, were a large carpet warehouse and the premises from which was distributed Rowland's Macassar Oil, long famous as a hair-dressing for men. This was a great boon to drapers, creating a demand for antimacassars which, by the end of the Victorian period, were in more general use as chairbacks even than the Macassar oil against which they were originally devised. Holborn was still a shopping street in mid-century but, more significant for the future, were the premises in Tottenham Court Road of such eventually famous names as Shoolbred, Maple's and of a widow and her son called Heal. All three originally catered for the drapery, fabrics and furniture requirements of nearby Bloomsbury. Oxford Street was already a flourishing shopping street. There were already a successful haberdasher called Peter Robinson, the drapery store of Marshall & Snelgrove and, behind Oxford Street, Debenham's had already long been established in Wigmore Street.

In view of its relative modernity and its proximity to Mayfair, Regent Street was already more fashionable, and was to stay

Shopping in Regent Street, 1884

more fashionable, than Oxford Street. Although not many of its first shops were long enduring successes, Jay's, near Oxford Circus, founded in the 1830s, was the outstanding London store to minister to the Victorian rituals of mourning. Their assistants and dressfitters would travel to all parts free of expense, taking with them 'Dresses, Mantles and Millinery besides Patterns of Materials, all marked in Plain Figures and at the same price as if purchased at the warehouse'. (It may be noted that as late as 1890 this distinguished establishment was still describing itself by the soon-to-be-downgraded label 'warehouse'). Regent Street's other really famous shop had been there since the street was built; this was Swan and Edgar's, enjoying the considerable advantage of its corner site at Piccadilly Circus and what, in its original form, was regarded as a handsome building. Then, as later, Bond Street had shops of the highest class, though in the 1850s it still also had a large number of aristocratic town houses; Piccadilly had already had Fortnum and Mason's since the first decade of the eighteenth century and, further west still, the name of Harvey had already appeared over a shopfront in Knightsbridge.

None of these establishments was, in the 1850s, the department store that most of them were to become by the twentieth century; they all prided themselves principally upon their specialisation and their favourite customers were 'the carriage trade'. All who called by carriage to arrange their purchases were excessively fawned upon, particularly by the shopwalker who, since he ministered to and profited from, the frailty of the female fancy and thus involved husbands in bills they doubtless regarded as unnecessarily expensive, was one of the most disliked characters in society; in contrast, head waiters, since they dealt with men, were felt to be altogether finer fellows. The nearest approach to a department store in early Victorian

94

London was really no more than a superior version of the street markets. These were the bazaars where, under one large roof, there was a variety of stalls offering millinery, cutlery, toys, ornaments and various forms of knick-knackery. Among such establishments were the Soho Bazaar in Soho Square, just north of Carlisle Street, and the Pantheon Bazaar in Oxford Street; and, in Belgrave Square, the Pantechnicon, which specialised mainly in the sale of every kind of carriage.

The pioneer of the departmental store in London was the indefatigable Yorkshireman, William Whiteley, who in 1863 decided to start up in suburbia, in Westbourne Grove, not far from Paddington station and the fashionable areas of Bayswater and Tyburnia, and not much further away from prosperous Kensington Park. Within 5 years the Circle line was to provide an underground station (Bayswater) within a few minutes walk of his premises, a factor hardly less important for Whiteley's trade than the Metropolitan station at Gower Street (Euston Square) was for Shoolbred's. Whiteley began by building up an unusually wide variety of drapery and clothing departments and in a few years had a whole row of Westbourne Grove shops.

Afternoon shoppers at Whiteley's in Westbourne Grove, 1900; the carriage trade is much in evidence

By 1872, he had departments for dressmaking, gentlemen's outfitting, tailoring, boots and hats. He soon styled himself 'The Universal Provider'; he started a house agency, a refreshment room, and a cleaning and dyeing service, and went on to sell stationery, furniture, china and glass and ironmongery. He branched out into house-decorating and hairdressing and a banking deposit service; and such was the growth of his business that he took over houses in nearby streets as living-in quarters for his staff. Westbourne Grove became thronged with the well-to-do and the fashionable. Whiteley's rapidly became a place where you could buy a house and furnish it, and feed and clothe yourself until at last you died, whereupon Whiteley's funeral department could do all that was necessary.

Whiteley's success had a considerable effect on the development of department stores elsewhere in London. The earliest were the Civil Service Supply Association started in 1865 and the Army and Navy Stores in Victoria Street in 1872. The latter owed something of its early success to one of Whiteley's former employees, the most famous of whom, however, was Richard Burbridge who, after being head of Whiteley's provision department, was to transform Harrod's from a one-man grocery shop into a store with an annual turnover of £250,000 by 1889; a former Whiteley employee was also associated with the early days of the Kensington store of John Barker. Closer rivals in his own Westbourne Grove were the Ponting's drapery store which eventually moved into Kensington High Street alongside Barker's, and William Owen, whose own drapery and department store on the north side of Westbourne Grove competed with Whiteley's until it closed down soon after the end of the First World War. In 1878 he faced the further competition of the newly opened store of Gamage's in Holborn which was to survive until 1972.

In 1880, however, Whiteley had extended his operations into Queen's Road itself. The public were offered 9 new departments: they could henceforth buy their wines and spirits, beers, flowers, pictures, fish and railway tickets at Whiteleys; and Whiteley's vans made two deliveries a day to inner London and one to the suburbs. There was a hire department which was so famous for the variety of the tasks it undertook that Whiteley himself was fond of recounting how, when a facetious clerical gentleman asked to be provided with an elephant, he had one delivered to the customer's stables within 4 hours. Queen Victoria herself patronised the shop, though not in person, since Her Majesty did not herself go shopping: a courier took her orders to the shop, which then sent the goods to Buckingham Palace by special messenger. Other members of the Royal Family visited Whiteley's in person, sometimes, though not always, incognito: they included the future Queen Alexandra and her son, the future George v.

Whiteley gradually overtook Shoolbred's, otherwise the greatest name in late Victorian shopping, chiefly because whereas Shoolbred's tended to emphasise quality in order to attract a largely aristocratic clientèle, Whiteley, though always noted for sound quality, made a wider appeal by his association of quality with cheapness. In the 1890s he forced the LGOC to run a bus service from Camden Town to Westbourne Grove by instituting a 12-minute bus service of his own until they gave in to his wishes. Despite the growing competition of Harrod's, his emporium reached its largest extent, employing a staff of 6,000. His hire department undertook mammoth assignments: a charity Ice Carnival at the Albert Hall under Royal patronage was managed by Whiteley's and collected three thousand guineas (£3,150) in admission money; in 1895 he supplied an Indian prince with an entire railway and a fleet of steamboats; and on Jubilee Day, 1897, he decorated the Royal Insurance Company's office in St James's Street from top to bottom in box-pleated strips of pink and white material, above which there was inscribed in letters of burnished copper, 'Thou art alone the Queen of Earthly Queens'.

The advent of departmental stores spread the idea of the 'fashionable' among the middle classes, previously concerned mainly with durability. They also cultivated a certain glamour. Also significant, because not confined to London, was the development of the multiple shop in the last quarter of the century. Already by the early 1890s, Thomas Lipton, a close friend both of Whiteley and the Prince of Wales, had opened 70 grocery shops in London in 3 years and was soon emulated by the International Tea Company's stores, the Home and Colonial, the Maypole Dairies, and, in the field of footwear, Freeman, Hardy and Willis; Sainsbury's too, had begun business in 1869, and Jesse Boot had as much impact on chemists' shops as Lipton's on the grocers'. But it was not until the end of the reign that branded, packaged and more or less prepared 'lines' became at all usual even in grocery shops, other than the multiples. In the small grocer's shops, treacle was only just beginning to be sold in tins, and flour, sugar, currants and tea no longer being stocked in the shops in barrels, chests and large containers, to be weighed out as and when the customer required. But already the names of Beecham, Cadbury and Fry were nationally known and nationally advertised, and patronised by the middle class and better-off artisan.

Further Reading
Dorothy Davis, *A History of Shopping*, 1966
A. W. Lambert, *The Universal Provider: William Whiteley*, 1938
The works of Mayhew and Booth cited at the end of Chapter 2
Hippolyte Taine, *Notes on England, 1872*, trans Edward Hyams, 1957

V

A Contrast of Suburbs

Superficially, a Victorian suburb was one that was largely
built-up between 1837 and 1901; but although this is a definition that excludes suburbs created in the twentieth century, it
still leaves too many to be described in one small book. It
seems, therefore, more helpful to look at just two of the many
possible areas that might have been examined. One chosen
area is the East End; the other is the northern part of Kensington, in the west of London. Though both of the areas selected
are north of the Thames, they are almost as widely separated
geographically as is possible when considering Victorian
London. Both were, and remain, 'problem' areas largely
because of what happened to them in Victorian times and
both were unusually varied in character. They differ in that
the East End had a history before the Victorian age, whereas
North Kensington had virtually none.

In the seventeenth century, many prosperous citizens had
houses in the rural parts of Stepney. In Hackney, Samuel
Pepys had seen orange trees in bloom in a garden in Lower
Clapton Road. Much of the East End remained fragrant and
delightful, with elm trees and winding lanes in the eighteenth
century. The suburban, if not semi-rural, character of the
East End, which is most accurately described as consisting
of Stepney, Poplar, Bethnal Green and, less certainly, Hackney,
but not Shoreditch, and certainly not Bermondsey on the south
side of the river, may be gauged by the fact that when the
London Hospital was built between 1752 and 1759 in the
Whitechapel Road, it was felt that its situation was too
rurally remote.

99

Early Victorian street scene near Hoxton, circa *1841*

The pre-Victorian East End was dominated by the river and, before Victoria became Queen, had no need for the straight roads that were to be created in the early nineteenth century. Cable Street was largely unbuilt and there was no Commercial Road, though Ratcliff Highway was *in situ* since, with its adjoining courts and alleys, it enabled sailors to spend their money in their own special ways. One turning, called Tiger Bay, was so-called because of its lurid 'Tigresses'. Shadwell had always been among the poorest of the hamlets, as was the small district of Limehouse just beyond Ratcliff, whose Chinese settlement dated only from the early nineteenth century. The Chinese, like the Indians, came to the East End largely owing to a shortage of manpower during the Napoleonic wars, the Indians settling mainly in Cable Street and Commercial Road. Poplar and Blackwall, the farthest away, were dependent upon the East India Company's moorings and building-slips, well before East India Docks were constructed in 1805–06. The Isle of Dogs was in 1800 a flat meadow and there were 7 windmills along the embankment at Millwall, creating an almost Dutch landscape.

Hackney Wick, which was mainly a Victorian development, was certainly of the East End, but Hackney proper was only doubtfully so owing to its respectable eighteenth-century history. Three miles (5 km) from London, healthy and agreeable, with views towards Epping across the Lea valley, it was still a respectable suburban area in Victorian times and well into the middle of the century the Loddiges brothers had a famous nursery in Hackney. When the nursery closed down, its celebrated palm tree, which had begun its career at Fontainebleau under the care of the Empress Josephine, was conveyed to Sydenham for replanting at Crystal Palace. The tree was then 50 feet (15 m) high and the cart on which it was set was pulled by 32 horses; its progress was a major public spectacle.

Multi-racial unloading of a tea ship from China at the London Docks, 1877

It was the building of the great East India Docks that began the history of expansion and urbanisation in the East End. The process was accelerated by the construction of the Eastern Counties Railway in 1839, the Blackwall Railway in 1840, the line from Bow via Stepney into Fenchurch Street in 1849, and by the North London extension to Broad Street in 1851. The construction of the docks attracted much labour to the district, as did the railways. The docks were a source of wonder and fascination to all who visited them. Mayhew found Dockland a place of tall chimneys vomiting clouds of black smoke. He noted the many-coloured flags flying the air, and how the air was pungent with fumes of rum and tobacco, now filled with the stench of hides, and now with the fragrance of coffee and spice. The dark vaults offered the mingled aromas of stored wines and the fungus smell of dry rot. There was a jumble of sounds on the docks, of 'boisterous nigger songs from the Yankee ship just entering', of the hammering of the coopers at their casks on the quay, of the chains of cranes rattling as they flew up again after casting loose their loads, of the splash of ropes in the water; of the shouted orders of a ship's captain with his mouth cupped in his hand, of empty casks being rolled along the stones with a sound like heavy drums. He observed how, while some heavily laden ships lay far down below the quay, others rode high up out of the water.

Taine writes:

> The docks are prodigious, overwhelming; there are six of them, each a great port and each inhabited by a population of three-masted ships. Always, ships, ships and more ships, lying side by side, showing the swelling lines of their prows, like handsome fishes in their copper sheathing. One is from Australia and displaces 2,500 tons; others are of 3,000 or more, and they come from every corner of the world. Most of them are magnificent; standing close under the hulls, they are leviathans, graceful and elegant as swans. A merchant who had come to check the arrival of spices from Java and a trans-shipment of ice from Norway, told me that about forty thousand ships enter these docks every year and that as a rule there are between five and six

thousand in the docks of the river at any given moment.

Every morning, the principal entrances of these Docks would be besieged by men seeking the casual employment that was the principal form of dock-workers' employment. It was, said Mayhew, 'a sight to sadden the most callous, to see thousands of men struggling for only one day's hire; the scuffle being made the fiercer by the knowledge that hundreds out of the number there assembled must be left to idle the day out in want'.

As well as the docks, the East End had huge sugar refineries and, though here the conditions of employment were better than the average, breweries, notably Truman's. As the century proceeded, larger scale manufacture moved away from the Whitechapel and Bethnal Green areas towards Bow Common, Old Ford and Hackney Wick, notably the unpleasant dye, glue and chemical works. Bryant and May's match factory was established by the river Lea and the river acquired an opaque colour and a 'urinous smell'. The Isle of Dogs and Millwall became centres for ironworks, and turpentine refining. Iron ships had been built on Thames-side near Bow since the beginning of the Queen's reign and the fitting and repair of ships had been undertaken at Blackwall. Between 3,000 and 4,000 men were employed in the Thames-side shipbuilding industry.

A turning point in the history of the riverside East End was the financial crisis of 1867 when work came to a standstill owing to bad weather and the shipyard workers and dock-workers, when better weather came, went on strike for more pay. The immediate result was the transfer of much ship-building to the Clyde, a blow from which the Thames-side shipbuilding was never to recover. Ratcliff, Wapping and Shadwell were never to regain their former vitality. Similarly, railway building, by displacing workers and overcrowding the area, drove from the East End all who could afford to live away from a district now not only overcrowded but clouded in soot. The respectable houses rapidly passed into multiple occupation; even those built as late as the early decades of the nineteenth century suffered this fate. This is a reminder that the Victorians often made slums rather than actually built them. Some large houses were turned over to factory use. Those houses which had originally, in conformity with pre-Victorian practice, been built with basements had their area caged in with iron bars. In the streets where there were smaller houses, they were usually equipped with window boxes and a door step, religiously scrubbed white.

The poorest interiors of the East End and its environs were fully described at various times in the Victorian age because they made the most sensational and horrific reading; but in that century, as since, the homes of the less poverty-stricken and the more stable elements in the ranks of the 'labouring poor' received little attention. They might have created the unwelcome impression that the difference between the better-off members of the so-called working class and the less comfortable among the middle class was not quite as great as it has always been fashionable to pretend, both among the middle class, who desired to go slumming out of a sense of moral righteousness, and among those to whom any member of 'the working classes' who adopted middle-class habits was something suspiciously like a traitor to the workers' cause.

Late-Victorian Limehouse interior: the kitchen range has a flat-iron resting on it and, on the right, artificial flowers under a glass dome. A 'poor' home but lovingly be-fringed and bedecked with ornaments

Mayhew was, on the whole, rather better than most in finding decent households among the labouring classes, actually confessing to come across, from time to time, East End households where a savoury-smelling stew dinner was being prepared, where the bedstead was furnished with a lively patchwork quilt and the dresser well and tidily furnished with clean plates and dishes. There might be chintz curtains, even though they would like as not be secondhand; and both curtains and bedspreads would be trimmed with a (secondhand) fringe. It was also a custom among the more prosperous East Enders to cover the walls with prints. The Irish naturally went in for saints; cats and children were also popular. A caged bird was almost a necessity and there were usually a few of the 'trashy' ornaments (china shepherdesses, lambs and shells were common) which so offended the Booth investigator when seen for sale in the markets. East Enders shared the customary better-off working-class family's pleasure in flowers, either in a tiny patch of garden or in a window box. Mignognette and plants of musk were sold in the streets by the hundreds of thousands in London streets during the summer. All these people were either exiles from the countryside, or had had their rural environment built upon by the advance of industrial London. In many ways, indeed, the solidly proletarian tradition of such areas as Wapping (and, south of the river, Bermondsey) provided a far more stable background than the isolated area in Kensington far away to the west that made up Notting Dale, which was cut off on all sides from a supporting and settled proletarian way of life.

Uncertainty of employment, not to mention the ravages of cholera, was such as to make even this most modest sort of prosperity uncertain. And apart from those in fairly regular work, the East End had its full quota of temporary or unsavoury occupations. There were teams of coal whippers, who unloaded the coal boats from Newcastle, the ballast heavers, who unloaded gravel, and the coal-backers who unloaded the barges from the Midland and Lancashire coalfields at the Regent's Canal Dock, all of them by the nature of their work tough, close-knit, hard-drinking men and all, like dockers, employed on a casual basis. Along the riverside, where, by mid-Victorian times, nobody any longer hired a boat for

East Enders set off from London Bridge by night for the Kentish hopfields, 1891

pleasure, there were purveyors who moved legally among the ships in the Pool selling drink, and others who sold it illegally. On the foreshore, scruffy children operated as 'mudlarks' combing the mud for anything that might be saleable, with the boys likely to end up as thieves and the girls as prostitutes. These last were mainly sought out by sailors, on the relatively short periods when they were in port, in the poverty-stricken area round the Ratcliff Highway, between the St Katharine and London Docks and Rosemary Lane. Here, too, were old women, knee deep in piles of rubbish on bits of wasteground, hoping to find something of value. There were men whose trade was to get into the sewers to scavenge; the activities of these 'toshers' were illegal and hazardous, and menaced by ferocious rats and the danger of drowning when the sewers were flooded by a high tide. There were also 'pure-finders' who collected dog's dung and sold it to be used in the process of dressing leather. Gaunt children collected cigar ends, or perhaps old bits of bread which would be soaked in water in order to give substance to a dish of oatmeal.

Poplar, Bromley and Bow all had some open spaces into the late 1840s and there were fields north of Whitechapel as late as the 1830s. But the population of Bromley, which had risen from 1,684 to 6,154 between 1801 and 1841, went up to 24,062 in the following 20 years. It expanded southwards towards Limehouse, and was built over with premises devoted to the production of varnish, grease and naphtha, particularly along the Limehouse Cut, once an attractive waterway. Poplar perhaps retained a middle-class element longer than Bow, and so did the fringes of Stepney and Bethnal Green, possibly as the dwelling places of clerical and managerial employees of the Docks.

Hackney expanded towards Clapton in a number of streets of semi-detached villas, and, in a more traditional kind of terraced housing, southwards towards Dalston, creating an area in which East Enders who rose in the world aspired to live. Their principal railway station was Dalston Junction; and their most distinguished and exceptional place of open-air recreation was Victoria Park, laid out in the 1840s with funds accruing to the Crown from the sale of York House, on open ground previously littered with brickfields, gravel pits and market gardens and once known as Bishop Bonner's Field. Its designer was a pupil of John Nash, James Pennethorne, who hoped to create a gracious setting for Victoria Park in order to attract the well-to-do. However, sufficient funds were not forthcoming, and from the start it was clear that wealthy Londoners would not buy building plots for houses in its neighbourhood. Relatively small in size, Victoria Park was made as varied as possible by Pennethorne, with facilities for bathing in two bathing lakes, and with plenty of contrast between attempts to perpetuate the much-admired English notion of the wilderness garden with shrubberies and trees, and areas set aside for ornamental flower beds—'carpet gardening' as it was called. This was much admired by East Enders, condemned as they were to a daily environment of

Victoria Park, Hackney, shortly after its opening

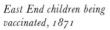
East End children being vaccinated, 1871

the higgledy-piggledy and the dingy. The most widely celebrated part of Victoria Park, however, was the stretch of ground which came to be used as a public meeting place. It was not, like Speakers' Corner in Hyde Park, for licensed eccentrics but for more serious purposes. East End Missions had gatherings there; the Moody and Sankey revival manifested itself vigorously in the Park, and disputes raged between Christians and the dreaded National Secularist Society. Chartists of 1848, the Social Democratic Federation, and in particular the Dockers, from the time of their 1889 strike onwards, made it their open forum.

The music hall tradition, as it eventually grew up, certainly developed in part out of the East End habit of musical evenings held in the pubs, when the range of songs sung would include dockers' work-songs and shanties, and songs imported by the Irish so effectively that sentimental ballads about Irish colleens and mothers may be regarded as an absolutely essential ingredient of English 'working-class culture'. Mayhew reported that dustmen were regular frequenters of the 'theaytre' in Leman Street and East End Jews regularly went to 'various' East End playhouses and cheap concerts, which Mayhew found very superior in quality to the 'trash and jingle which delights the costermonger class'. The cheapest form of entertainment was to be had at the so-called 'penny gaffs' which were makeshift theatres in converted warehouses, or similar premises, where 200 to 300 spectators could be crammed in. Regarded as morally objectionable, they flourished in the fifties and sixties, and seem to have attracted young audiences of a highly undisciplined character. The usual offering consisted of two 20-minute plays, with a song in the interval between them. The audience would show disapproval by throwing missiles on to the stage and its approval by throwing halfpennies instead. The plays usually had melodramatic themes, with titles such as *Seven Steps to Tyburn*, or the *Bloodstained Handkerchief*. In the streets, there was a plethora of buskers and, for special national occasions, the street tea party, a tradition somewhat self-consciously revived for the victory celebrations of 1919 and 1945 as well as for the Silver Jubilee of George v and Queen Mary in 1937.

The East End scene was always noisy and vulgar and perhaps seemed the more so as the century proceeded when, as soon as there was a little more money about, clothing began to become rather more garish. Costers had always tried to dress characteristically, being particularly proud of their boots; and the younger women gradually took over from the tarts (and their middle-class betters) the habit, if they could afford it, of wearing clothes of a shriekingly violent colour, set off by a shawl of a non-matching but equally strong colour in cold weather. Ostrich plumes were a concomitant of Sunday-best when this could be afforded, and one of the impressions of the East End working class (and not of the East Enders only) in the late nineteenth century was that some of the women, particularly the married ones, often seemed so much larger and more loud-mouthed than their menfolk. This phenomenon continued into the early twentieth century and was not solely due to the fact that the women wore such mountains of clothing. The working-class woman whose apron was a piece of old sack and whose headgear was a male cloth cap was once a reality and not just an imaginative fiction thought up by Donald Gill for seaside picture postcards.

Some working-class households were matriarchal to a degree even at a time when the middle-class stereotype of the married woman was that of a submissive object. The poor working girl forever being given a black eye by her 'feller', her 'bloke' or her 'old man' naturally received most attention from social investigators because that is what they expected to find; equally, the frail women weighed down by a succession of unwanted pregnancies or deserted by an oafish man, would be instantly comprehensible to the ladies who went 'slumming'.

But the popularity of music hall songs such as Gus Elen's *It's a Great Big Shame* (not been married not a month nor more, When underneath her thumb goes Jim, O isn't it a pity that the likes of 'er Should put upon the likes of 'im) is a reminder that there was quite another type of East End working-class woman, the virago. Nor was it merely men who brawled drunkenly outside public houses. The spectacle of two beer-sodden women yelling and shouting at each other and pulling each other's hair out by the handful was one of the more alarming incidents to be met with in parts of the Victorian East End.

If one turns from the East End to consider an inner suburban area to the west of London, there can be no greater contrast than that provided by the area sharply bounded on the west,

Map of Kensington, 1841

in fact if not officially, by the virtually defunct West London Railway and now, even more brutally, by the M41 motorway, and on the east by the beginnings of Bayswater. Bounded on the south by the present Holland Park Avenue and Notting Hill Gate, it stretches as far north as the Harrow Road and is, administratively, North Kensington. This name it acquires by virtue of constituting the northern part of the old parish of Kensington and then, from 1899 to 1963, of the Royal Borough of Kensington, and thereafter of the Royal Borough of Kensington and Chelsea.

North Kensington differs from the East End in that at the beginning of Victoria's reign it was almost all open farmland so that virtually all of it was built over between 1840 and 1902. The fact that it was built over so late, was so thinly populated even after the Victorian period began, and had such marked social differences within it from the start has always made it difficult for its inhabitants, let alone those who governed it from far away to the south of Holland Park, to think of it as having a single identity. Thus, various, though differing, parts of it have been called Notting Hill. Its northernmost area was for long referred to by the name of the principal, long-surviving Notting (or Notten) Barns Farm in those parts; though the immediate environs of the farm, when first built on, became St Quintin Park. With other parcels of the North Kensington area being called Notting Dale, Westbourne Park, Kensington Park and Kensal New Town, it can be guessed that, from the beginning, the various parts of it had different social and environmental circumstances.

In the early years of the nineteenth century, the only features of note in North Kensington, apart from the Notten Barns and Portobello Farms, were the Kensington Gravel Pits, and the Piggeries and Potteries. The Kensington Gravel Pits were immediately east of the northern end of Kensington Church Street and gave their name to the small village which grew up around them and to the turnpike on the main east-west road, then variously known as the Great Road from Tyburn to Uxbridge or the Oxford Road. Further west, much nearer Shepherds Bush, a brickfield, begun in the late eighteenth century, still survived into Victorian times, employing a number of Irish labourers. On this brickfield there arose a pottery whose kilns were the solitary feature marked on a map of 1833 and which produced tiles, flower pots and drainpipes. To the brickworkers and pottery workers were added, after 1820, a colony of pig-keepers, living on small plots of land and collecting kitchen waste in horse and donkey carts from houses or hotels in the West End. They would turn the stuff over when they got home, eat the best of it, sell some of it to their neighbours, boil down the fat and give what remained to their pigs. This trafficking in the droppings from rich men's houses by the people of Notting Dale so long ago marked them as real-life antecedents of those late twentieth century horse-and-cart characters, Steptoe and Son, whose creators had thus provided them with an historically apt location in much the same part of London.

Cottages in Kensington Potteries, 1855

The Piggeries and Potteries were a quite isolated colony at the beginning of the reign and were not much less so at the end of it. The brick-makers could earn good money in summer, but might be penniless in winter. They sustained themselves for their 15-hour working day with large quantities of beer and their wives and children worked alongside them in the thick wet clay. Conditions among the Piggeries, where, in some 260 hovels, there were said to be over 3,000 pigs and 1,000 humans, were described in Chadwick's 1849 Report as 'filthy in the extreme'. As may be imagined, given the complete lack of sanitation and the large number of pigs, all the well water was contaminated. Dickens described the Potteries as 'a plague spot scarcely equalled in insalubrity by any other part of London'. The inhabitants were severely hit by the cholera epidemics, by a scarlet fever epidemic of 1870 and by the influenza epidemic of 1889–90, the first to sweep the country for several decades. Notting Dale, as the district was by now being called, was shown to have a higher death rate from smallpox than anywhere else in Kensington and of every 50 deaths, 43 were of children under 5. The pig-keeping district continued to spread southwards and also westwards to the West London Railway line, and Charles Booth's investigations showed that, in the 1890s, infant mortality rates there were as high as in the 1850s. At the end of the reign, half the children born in the district died before they were 1 year old, there was 1 public house for every 25 houses, and there were scores of squalid lodging houses as well as furnished rooms let for overnight use. It was a part of London that all but the most dedicated social workers took pains to avoid throughout and long after the Victorian age.

This sorry tale, which was only the beginning of the long story of North Kensington's pockets of poverty, was a striking contrast to other early Victorian developments nearby. One false start which was soon halted and left virtually no trace behind was the establishment of the Hippodrome racecourse in 1837 covering some 200 acres stretching from the Potteries to the present Portobello Road and as far north as where the Hammersmith and City line was later to run. Intended as a rival to Epsom and Ascot, it had barely one successful season and was abandoned after 1841.

The first important building project to be completed was on the north side of what the plans still called 'the High Road leading from Notting Hill to Shepherds Bush' and just east of where the M41 motorway now runs. It consisted of Norland (now Royal) Crescent, Queen's (now Queensdale) Road, Norland Square, St James's Square and St Ann's Villas and included a handsome church, dedicated to St James and consecrated in 1845. Many of the houses in this new Norland Town were in two-storeyed pairs, but the crescent and other terraced streets show by their design and ornament a determination to produce frontages less austere than those of the traditional London squares. All this was high-class property, in keeping with the trend of the first 20 years of the reign to construct a great wedge of high-quality residences from Belgravia into South Kensington and along the whole northern length of Hyde Park. But the building schemes in Norland Town were over-ambitious for the time. The area was too far away from the West End and too near the Potteries. Builders repeatedly went bankrupt and, from the beginning, those parts of Norland Town which were closest to the Potteries were quickly turned into multi-occupied slums, despite the efforts made by the planners of the estate to make direct access from the Potteries as difficult as possible.

Although projected earlier, the more impressive Ladbroke estate was longer in the completion and more extensive. The spine of the original estate was Ladbroke Grove, and its focal point, built on high ground, St John's Church. The crescents, gardens and squares constructed in this area, west of Kensington Park Road and as far north as Elgin Crescent, all built approximately between the 1830s and 1860, were remarkable, at least in the parts nearest Holland Park, for the large size of their paired villas and for the scenic quality of the many terraces and crescents. Over much of the estate, the gardens were very large and the frontages of the houses wider than those in other parts of London. Many of the facades were over-rich and too flamboyant for architectural purists, but 'leafy Ladbroke' was one of the most attractive upper-class suburban areas in Victorian London. Its standing may be judged by the fact that Galsworthy thought it worthy to provide a suitable home for old Nicholas Forsyte of whom it

The Ladbroke estate, Notting Hill: Stanley Crescent and Kensington Park Gardens, based on a drawing made by the architect

was recorded 'he had made a large fortune, quite legitimately, out of the companies of which he was a director'. There is no suggestion that Galsworthy thought that part of Ladbroke Grove a less desirable place of residence than Stanhope Gate, Park Lane, Hyde Park Mansions, the Bayswater Road or Campden Hill where the other wealthy Forsytes lived.

The influence of the Ladbroke estate was carried eastward, though on a much less ambitious scale, beyond Kensington Park Road, towards Bayswater, and south of Westbourne Grove to include Chepstow Villas, Pembridge Villas and Square by the 1860s. Most of the houses here have wider frontages than is usual in London. There was thus created in 'Kensington Park' a large number of handsome, generous houses, most of which still survive. But there were practical reasons why this building, taken over all, covered only a limited portion of North Kensington. The very low density of the earliest part of the Ladbroke estate proved too uneconomic to be maintained even in Kensington Park itself. By the mid-1860s house-building for the more prosperous middle class had outrun demand. For a long time, Ladbroke Grove itself stopped short of the south side of where the Hammersmith and City line was to run. Attempts to be more ambitious in the less accessible areas, as in Colville and Powis Squares beyond the Portobello Road were unsuccessful financially almost from the start and the houses in both were among the first in North Kensington to be divided up into multiple occupancy. Remoteness from the Bayswater Road, the proximity of the teeming Portobello Road street market which grew up at about the same time, together with the excess of houses over purchasers, all helped to explain the poor quality of the building between Westbourne Grove and Westbourne Park stations.

Proximity to Notting Dale had a similar effect on the housing within the area around Latimer Road station. By the end of the century the Notting Dale and Latimer Road area had coalesced into an overcrowded enclave populated in part by sober hardworking people and in part by characters of the most dubious sort. West of the Latimer Road, the West London Railway was unbridged; not until the last part of the reign was there even a road leading out into the Uxbridge Road at Shepherds Bush. As for Notting Dale itself, that too was blocked, to the south by the back of the Norland estate, and on the east by the success of the builders of the Ladbroke estate in seeing there was virtually no access to it from the Potteries. To the north, almost to the end of the reign, was nothing but common land stretching up to the Great Western Railway and the Paddington Canal.

The character of the Dale and Latimer Road did change a little by the end of the reign. The pig-keepers were in part replaced by gypsies, and as a result of the slump in brick-building in the late 1860s, many of their wives took in washing, making the district in the end a veritable laundryland. Carpet beating was another characteristic of parts of North Kensington; and a century later the traveller on the Hammersmith and City line could still see a building in the Latimer Road area bearing the legend Patent Steam Carpet Beating Company. But it was a neighbourhood desperately in need of civilising; and one of the most remarkable features of North Kensington was the large number of churches and chapels and mission halls which had been established there by the end of the reign. It was also well supplied with schools by the London School Board and had even acquired a small open space called Avondale Park. The historian of Notting Hill who thought that the people of Notting Dale and Latimer Road were not quite as bad as they were usually made out to be was perhaps not far wrong.

Ladbroke Grove, corner of Lancaster Road, 1866, with the Metropolitan line at Notting Hill (now Ladbroke Grove) station in background. The grand manner of the Ladbroke Estate is not in evidence here

It can be seen that the socially divided character of North Kensington existed well before the coming of the Hammersmith and City line in 1864. Nevertheless the line had a deleterious effect on the area that was built over on either side of it to the east of Portobello 'Lane'. The triangle whose three sides are the Metropolitan and Great Western Railways and the Portobello Road was filled with good-sized lower middle-class houses occupied, at first, by 'superior mechanics and railway employees'; but this obviously did not last. The population of this small corner grew so rapidly that it was the first part of North Kensington to have a board school built for it. It was further turned in on itself by being denied by the Paddington Canal Company direct road access across the canal into the Harrow Road. Accordingly, by the end of the reign it was already depressed and depressing, having access only to the dreariest northern part of Portobello Road or with the even more rundown area of Kensal New Town, while for the most part being hemmed in by railways and a canal.

On the other hand, the Metropolitan may have stimulated development north of the railway and west of Ladbroke Grove in the St Charles's Ward. The opening of the elementary school in Oxford Gardens by the London School Board in 1884 gives a clue as to the character of this area. The local tradesmen who petitioned for the school's establishment asked that the fee be as high as possible in order to keep it 'select'. Until 1891, when fees in board schools were abolished, Oxford Gardens' pupils paid 6d (2½p) a week which was much nearer the statutory maximum of 9d (4p) than can have been the fees charged (if they were charged at all) in the nearby schools in Latimer Road, Lancaster Road, and Sirdar Road, let alone the Golborne schools at Portobello Road and Wornington Road to the north west. The 'superiority' of this particular school was preserved for most of its history as an elementary school.

The northern part of St Charles's Ward, along the axis of the extended Ladbroke Grove, fared as badly as did every other property development that did not have quick access to the prosperous residential or business parts of London. St Charles's Square, built opposite the Catholic young men's college of St Charles, opened by Cardinal Manning, Archbishop of Westminster, in 1874, began as an almost aristocratic quarter. It acquired a convent and the redbrick edifice of St Marylebone Infirmary in 1891. These institutional buildings imparted a certain gloom to the neighbourhood, made worse by the erection of working-class houses by small builders immediately north of the square which attracted an overspill both from Kensal New Town and Notting Dale.

Thus, to walk the near 2-mile (3-km) length of Ladbroke Grove at the end of the reign, was to make a pilgrimage through most of the social gradations of Victorian London. Starting at its northern end in what was, until the Second World War, the aristocratic proximity of Holland House, one of the greatest of the country's Whig houses, it rose, a spacious boulevard, to the heights of St John's Hill and Ladbroke's well-laid estate, flanked by broad crescents and somewhat heavily handsome squares and then descended physically and socially until, by the time it had reached low ground beyond Blenheim Crescent, it passed through a dejected area of poverty where it was linked by Westbourne Park Road with the Portobello estate on the east and by Lancaster Road with Notting Dale and Latimer Road on the west. At Ladbroke Grove station (Notting Hill station then) it began to support the late nineteenth-century equivalent of a twentieth-century shopping arcade, with respectable shops and a restaurant where one could eat à la carte or table d'hôte. Some semblance of gentility was preserved as it passed through Cambridge Gardens, Oxford Gardens and Bassett Road; but by the time it reached St Charles's Square it was approaching drabness once more. As it rose up the hill beyond the Eagle and Earl Percy public houses it sank still further in the social scale, until, disgraced on the west by a gasworks and on the east by the once isolated but always plebeian little streets of Kensal New Town, depressingly labelled not streets but 'Rows', it finally seemed to die of shame opposite The Plough public house in the Harrow Road, itself a thoroughfare as drab as it was unending. Unlike the East End, North Kensington had no existence when Victoria came to the throne; and whereas parts of the East End had to be rebuilt because of destruction by the Luftwaffe, North Kensington, one is almost tempted to say unluckily, escaped destruction in the Blitz. It illustrates also, perhaps on

Notting Dale worthies: the vicar, churchwarden and sidesmen of the parish of St Clement, Notting Dale, circa 1894

an exaggerated scale, the fact that the Victorians built far too few specifically working-class houses, so that it is a little unjust, as far as London is concerned, to say that the Victorians built slums. They were, indeed, considerable destroyers of London slums; many of the more dreadful courts and alleys in the inner areas disappeared as a result of railway building and street improvements. Lack of sufficient genuinely working-class houses led to the creation of slums by commercial builders who over-speculated in houses suitable for occupation by the classes which employed servants at a time when the expanding railway system was turning more and more of the heads of servant-employing households into commuters to outer suburbs. Thus, the process of inner suburban decay which faced the twentieth century was begun almost as soon as some of the inner suburbs were built. In this respect, the eastern side of London fared rather better, since the East End was largely, though not wholly, a working-class expansion of communities that were working class before the Victorian period began. Building over most of the eastern side of London reflected much less than did that on the western side the speculative builder's concentration on attracting a relatively limited upper middle-class clientèle that was continually being enticed further and further outwards from the centre by the expanding transport system.

Further Reading
Millicent Rose, *The East End of London*, 1951
Florence Gladstone, *Notting Hill in Bygone Days*, 1924, reprinted, with additional material by Ashley Barker, 1969
D. L. Olsen, *Town Planning in London in the 18th and 19th Centuries*, 1964
Hermione Hobhouse, *Thomas Cubitt, Master Builder*, 1971
H. J. Dyos, *Victorian Suburb. A Study of the Growth of Camberwell*, second edn., 1966. This is considered the most important academic study of suburban growth in the Victorian period so far to be published.
A Theatre of Suburbs. Some patterns of development in West London 1801–1911, D. A. Reeder (in *Studies in Urban History*, ed. H. J. Dyos, 1968)
Arthur Sherwell, *Life in West London*, 1901
S. Potter, *The Story of Willesden*
A. Montgomery Eyre, *St John's Wood*, 1913

VI

Woman: Dream and Reality

The model by which the Victorian woman was supposed to be guided was that provided by the Queen; and the style of family life to which the nation was urged to conform was that pursued by the Queen and Prince Albert until the Prince's untimely death in 1861. It is usual nowadays to suggest that the example provided by the Court and Royal Family owed more to Prince Albert than to the Queen herself. This is perhaps to overlook the fact that although the Queen had a fairly disreputable set of Royal uncles, she had, in George III and his Queen, highly respectable and decorous grandparents. True, the Queen had, as a young woman, a tendency to be boisterous and flighty whereas the Prince was reserved, sensitive, cultivated and artistic; but she would hardly have remained so faithful to his memory and his standards for the 40 years after his death had she not entered so fully and willingly into their 20 years of domesticity together. The ideals, therefore, which the Court set before the nation were of absolute sexual 'purity' and of total absorption in family domesticity. As Taine wrote of the English middle class, 'It is obvious to me that, for them, happiness consists in that state: home at six in the evening, an agreeable, faithful wife, tea, four or five children clambering over their knees, and respectful servants'.

Adequate though this may be as a generalisation it represents a way of life which, in London at any rate, was followed mainly by the respectable lower middle class and the better-off respectable working class. The two outstanding differences between London and elsewhere were that, like all great capital cities it was a playground for the rich, and that to a greater extent than most other European capitals it contained large areas of degrading poverty. Inevitably, therefore, London provided ample scope for the sexual irregularities of what Taine called 'the fouled hindquarters' of English life.

The phrase, however, is too coarse to be appropriate to the growing influence, after his marriage in 1863 to Princess Alexandra, of Edward, Prince of Wales and his friends, collectively referred to as 'The Marlborough House set', which, owing to the long period when the Queen refused to appear in public because of her condition as a grief-stricken widow, acted as a substitute for the Court. It was not simply that the Prince was gregarious and fond of gambling, horse-racing and women. The Princess of Wales herself was beautiful to begin with, and grew more beautiful with the years. She was graceful, forgiving and charming; whereas the widowed Queen, though formidably regal and sometimes gracious, was dumpy, frequently sentimental, often rather grumpy, wilfully eccentric and much given to not being amused (at any rate when anybody was looking; in private she could be quite merry). But although the contrast between the Queen and the Princess was one of

A garden party at Holland House, 1872: here, one may guess, are Taine's 'over-trimmed hats', 'too shiny' hair, and styles 'overfull, striped and fussed'

style and beauty, the contrast between the Queen and her Court and the Prince and his cronies was wider. Edward made horse-racing a royal sport once more (and actually made a profit on his own horses) and was for a long time a patron of private gambling. He made yachting fashionable too; and though he resolutely excluded the kind of low-lifers who hung round the Regency aristocrats, he hobnobbed with cosmopolitan financiers, actresses in both London and Paris, and even music hall 'artistes'. The result was to provide Victorian London 'Society' with more than one sensation. Thus, in 1870, Sir Charles Mordaunt, one of the Prince's set, sought a divorce from his 21-year old wife, who suddenly wrote to him that the blindness of her newly born child was due to her wickedness in committing adultery with a number of people including the Prince of Wales. The Prince had in fact written her a dozen letters. In the witness box he denied adultery but was not cross-examined. The petition was dismissed on the grounds of the wife's insanity, though a second petition, which did not name the Prince, succeeded later.

Edward also patronised Sarah Bernhardt from the 1880s onwards, a daring step, since 'actresses' had for long had the connotation that 'model' was later to have in Soho. He also created an actress: Lily Langtry, who played the lead in several West End plays solely because the Prince persuaded the Bancrofts to let her do so. Known as 'the Jersey Lily' her other intimate friends included a Habsburg Crown Prince, the King of the Belgians and two American citizens, one from Texas and another from Indiana. Even the pure-minded Gladstone allowed her to write to him, using the code sign that ensured the letter was not opened by his secretaries.

These and the many other adventures with women in which the Prince indulged were always a source of anxiety because they threatened to break down the elaborately maintained Victorian pretence that sexual behaviour outside the confines of monogamous marriage did not exist. And though there was, in practice, rather less pretence about the fact that postponement of marriage until a man could afford to support a wife, a large brood of children and a sufficient staff of domestics might well lead him to have recourse to 'low' women in his bachelor days, such behaviour was still deplored; and it did not make the women involved acceptable to the rest of society. Respectable women, therefore, would not go out alone by day unless they were married, and would not go out alone at night whether they were married or not, in order to avoid contact with, or the danger of being mistaken for, those 'unfortunates' whose profession it was to minister to men's 'baser passions'. It was rarely understood that social convention itself would, particularly in a teeming metropolis such as London was, make universal conformity to the official code extremely difficult. The more respectable and aristocratic a woman was, and the more aristocratic a man was, the less they were allowed to do except indulge in a social round which made flirtation or husband-chasing on the one side, and woman-chasing on the other, the only exciting occupation available, apart, in the case of men, from drink and various forms of sport. The various carryings-on of the Prince of Wales in London, in country houses all over England and among the demi-mondaines of Paris were very much the consequence of Queen Victoria's refusal to give him important state duties to perform, while constantly complaining that he was 'frivolous'.

What was true of the Prince applied to 'the leisured classes' in general, those people to whom Gladstone gloweringly applied the term 'the West End of London'. For the West End was indeed primarily the leisured classes' playground. The 'work' the men did was principally about their country estates or on the rural magistrates' bench. Even if they were engaged in national politics, this rarely occupied much of their time. By twentieth-century standards, politics was conducted by part-time amateurs, and so indeed was government. Lesser men and most of the women did little work that was not voluntary social work and apart from the relatively few, well-publicised exceptions (like Florence Nightingale, Baroness Burdett-Coutts, Octavia Hill and Beatrice Potter) they did most of that in the country. Inevitably, this trivialised the daily life of the upper classes in London and was largely responsible for calling into existence the middle-class gospel of work and self help which gave members of that class a justificatory creed as well as a standard of behaviour by which the really leisured classes could be criticised and judged.

This constant awareness that men of property who were also

merchants and professional men were sitting in judgment on them and probably finding them wanting all through the Victorian age made the leisured classes more than usually devious in their pursuit of amorous adventure and zealous in their attempts to pretend they did not exist. The result was that those who kept to the principal rule of the game, namely the pretence that they were not playing it, could continue undisturbed. This is illustrated by the various alarms caused by the too frequent signs that the Prince of Wales might be publicly exposed and by the sympathy that was extended to Princess Alexandra's gentle insistence that her husband's lady friends were indeed friends, but no more.

Yet one consequence of the secrecy veiling the realities was that many English girls of the upper classes felt unusually safe in male company. It was not essential to be timidly demure in the presence of a gentleman, since gentlemen were only 'ungentlemanly' in the presence of females who were not ladies. This could give girls of the upper classes an openness and free-dom of manner which startled Taine when he was in London. The considerable part of the year spent in the country by girls of the best families enabled them to present themselves for the London 'Season' from May to July with fresh, rosy com-plexions, strong limbs and the ability to sit firmly and hand-somely in the saddle. Taine thought it worthy of comment that they could be seen riding in Hyde Park (in the mornings) 'with no other company than that of a servant'. But this air of happy camaraderie notwithstanding, he noted that these healthy English girls engaged fairly resolutely in 'husband hunting'. The young, he noted, 'meet and mingle freely and without surveillance'. But that was one of the principal purposes of the London Season. It was not merely bright with public occasions such as the race meetings at Epsom (of which Derby Day was the one event in which the populace at large participated) and Ascot, the Royal Academy Exhibition and the University cricket match; these months of high summer were a time of Court balls, levees and garden parties and of balls, dances and receptions at all the aristocratic houses of London. This did not merely provide an ostentatious round of pleasure. The aim was also the serious one of finding husbands for young girls and brides for young men. And since marriages

Three Little Maids from below stairs,
circa *1874*

were not in the formal sense 'arranged' it was important that young people, with or without maternal pressures, should see, and be seen by, the potential marriage partners whom the Season so briefly brought into the capital from the best families in all the far-flung counties.

For the girls, therefore, the Season could be decisive. It was short; it would terminate abruptly with the coming of August. Not to find a husband after relatively few Seasons would be to find oneself 'on the shelf'. Few families lacked daughters who had not married; many relied heavily on their fulfilling the roles, successively, of helpful grown-up daughters, useful sisters-in-law and, finally, understanding maiden aunts. But the Victorian period, perhaps more than most, was not one in which it was pleasant for a woman to stay permanently unmarried.

Yet the system seemed to produce unusually faithful wives. Taine fell back on the theory that it was partly due to the aristocratic and upper middle-class habit of spending much of the year in the country, where they were freer from temptation.

It could have been due to their having so many children and thus such large staffs of domestic servants to supervise; to their interest in 'good works'; and to their habit of reading newspapers and reviews and serious books from the circulating libraries of which Mudie's was by far the most famous, buying one hundred and fifty thousand volumes a year. Unlike French writings, the English novel had a very high moral tone, studiously avoiding reference to sex. Mr Mudie, who had opened his Select Lending Library in 1842, indeed guaranteed that he would stock nothing that was not fit to be read by a delicately brought-up 16-year old girl. The most heavily borrowed volumes he stocked in the sixties were the works of the lady novelists, Charlotte M. Young, Mrs Henry Wood, Mrs Oliphant and Miss Braddon; and, despite her daring exposé of wickedness in high society, Ouida; though Mr Mudie made her works available only because public demand proved irresistible.

Almost the only concession to the physical qualities of womanhood was provided by the annual exhibitions of the Royal Academy, since this was the one occasion in the London year when the unclothed or nearly unclothed female body could be represented to the public gaze without arousing universal censure; though from time to time the occasional prelate felt moved to express the view that the proceedings were morally dangerous. Victorian painting devoted at least as much care to the depiction of the nude or the nearly-nude female body as to portraying stags at bay. But of course there were conventions about it. What Victorian art displayed was 'the female form in all its divine beauty' and almost invariably in settings derived from classical mythology which at once endowed them with respectability, so as to achieve what Sir Kenneth Clark, writing of Victorian nudes in general, has called 'the calculated avoidance of reality'. The most prolific of early-Victorian painters of nudes was William Etty, who has been described by one modern critic as possessing 'a luscious sense of form'. Like another contemporary painter of nudes, Gibson, whose *Painted Venus* of 1850 was thought insufficiently like a 'goddess' to incur a certain degree of censure, Etty was unmarried. Later celebrants of the female form were the revered Royal Academicians Lord Leighton (another bachelor) and Lawrence Alma-Tadema. Using such titles as *Venus Disrobing for the Bath* (1867) and *Ariadne Abandoned by Theseus* (1868) Leighton created a dream world in which lovely ladies swam before the eyes strategically protected by delicate draperies from accusations of impropriety, but miraculously preserving delicate English complexions under the blazing sun and cloudless blue of a Mediterranean sky. Victorian fashions contrived to make women appear as unreal when their clothes were on as paintings made them seem when they were off. The crinoline flourished for a relatively brief period in the 1860s, being replaced for most of the rest of the century by some form of that odd rear protuberance known as the bustle, which had indeed been introduced in the early 1830s. The crinoline had a certain charm; but for women to endure for long the manifest inconvenience of these hoop-like contrivances was to ask too much. The crinoline did, however, possess two valuable assets: it kept men at a distance but, judiciously manoeuvred, could tantalise them with fleeting glimpses of ankle and calf. For all that, Taine found London womankind deplorably deficient in dress sense when he surveyed them in Hyde Park:

> Crinolines too full, or the fullness badly draped, like geometrical cones or else dented; ribbons and scarves green; gold lacing; bold, flower patterned materials; a profusion of floating gauze; hair bunched, falling or curled. The whole display surmounted by tiny hats, much trimmed but hardly perceptible. The hats are over-trimmed, the hair too shiny and clamped to the temples with too hard a line; the *mantalet* or *casaque* hangs shapeless to the hips, the skirt is monstrously overfull and the whole of this scaffolding is badly put together, badly matched, striped, fussed, overdone, loud, excessively numerous colours each swearing at the others.

He considered only the women of the highest class to be exempt from the general conclusion that 'they get themselves up like bundles of rags'. He declared himself shocked by the sartorial excesses of the ladies and girls of the rich middle class he saw parading in the Park on Sundays: 'hats which look like sprays of rhododendron piled up in a heap . . . dresses of purple silk . . . or stiff tulle on a substructure of skirts bristling with embroidery . . . gold chains, gold belts with gold clasps; hair lying in a gleaming mass on the nape of the neck. The glare and glitter is brutal: they look as if they . . . are parading to display the wares of a fancy-goods shop. . . . As a result you do not see three pretty figures'.

Another source of distortion, apart from the sheer quantity of clothing Victorian women wore, was the corset, which throughout the century had the aim of constricting the waist. The consequence of doing this really effectively was often to make it impossible for women to breathe except from the upper part of the chest. This, together with the fact that corsets tended to push the breasts upwards, doubtless accounted for the frequency with which 'heaving bosoms' were referred to in Victorian novels and the prevalence of female fainting attacks. The passionate, suffering search after a 15-inch (37-cm) waist which Victorian fashion imposed can perhaps be explained by the fact that a feminine waist of such dimension could so easily be 'encircled' by the beloved, even if his own sleeve-length was relatively short; or by the impression of girlish immaturity it might convey, since in mid-century little girls were, not unexpectedly, much sentimentalised over by the many men upon whom adherence to the Victorian code had laid the burden of life-long sexual immaturity. But that fashionable women should go decidedly 'in' in their middles continued to be mandatory even when, doubtless under the influence of so much royal patronage from Marlborough House, the predominant style of beauty was heavily busted and large-bottomed. The Junoesque 'fine figure of a woman' of the 'Society' scene at the end of the reign, like the many huge-girthed men of the time, was probably also a product of the Victorian upper-class vice of over-eating. Cadbury's cocoa had, as one of its selling lines in the 1880s, the claim that it was 'flesh forming'.

The middle class was, on the whole, the class that took the Victorian code most seriously; and its response to fashion was somewhat sluggish until the coming of the department store. In mid-century it seemed to be possessed of more money than taste; but, being the middle class it had to avoid the accusations of excess or provocativeness. Thus, the further one descended the social scale the greater the tendency in the second half of the century to wear high-necked dresses almost as a form of silent protest against the shameless décolleté style of high fashion, where low-cut dresses exposed gleaming white shoulders and rather more of 'the figure' than was really proper.

Since it was held that (though it was bad) it was better for a young man to have recourse to prostitutes than to commit the heinous crime of marrying 'beneath him' socially, and since any overt amorous contact with a respectable member of the opposite sex, however slight, was forbidden by social convention, prostitution flourished. Estimates of numbers, being usually the work of indignant reformers, tended to be astronomical. Perhaps Sir John Simon's estimate of 18,000 in London may have been less unreliable than most; other estimates were 80,000 and 120,000; a medical authority on the subject assessed the total annual sum spent on prostitutes as £8 million. One difficulty is the tendency of observers to describe as a prostitute any female who was kept by a man, for however long or short a period of her life, without benefit of a marriage ceremony. This was one of the reasons why humble women attached such importance to their marriage certificate (their 'lines') as a testimony to their respectability. Thus any female Victorian, not born a member of the aristocracy, who had at any time sexual relations with someone other than a legally procured husband, tended to be regarded, and to regard herself, as a prostitute. Such comprehensiveness naturally gave great statistical scope to campaigners against this 'great social evil'.

At the very top of the profession, according to Mayhew, were 'kept mistresses and prima donnas'. The most celebrated of these in the Victorian age was Catherine Walters, known as Skittles or, to her closest friends, 'Skitsie', born in the dockside area of Liverpool in 1839. It is assumed she acquired her nickname from having earned money as a very young girl by working in a skittle alley in a Merseyside public house. She had, by the time she came to London in 1859, acquired exceptional skill as a horsewoman. This accomplishment resulted in her being employed in 1861 by the proprietor of a livery stable near Berkeley Square to advertise his horses by riding them, or driving them in a phaeton, in Hyde Park.

*'Skittles': dark-eyed
courtesan and
equestrienne, briefly
beloved of 'Harty-
Tarty' and bowed to by
Lord Kitchener*

Attired by her employer in a riding habit so closely moulded
to her figure that it had to be worn next to her skin, she was an
instant success in the Park. Sir Edwin Landseer's Royal Academy
painting of that year, *The Taming of the Shrew*, showed a
mettlesome horse being firmly handled by an exquisite young
horsewoman, instantly recognisable by the fashionable as none
other than Skittles herself. In 1862 she met (no one seems to
know how) young 'Harty-Tarty', the Marquis of Hartington,
became his mistress, was set up in a house in Mayfair, given a
life settlement of around £2,000 a year and publicly escorted
by her aristocratic lover at that year's Derby meeting. Thereafter, Skittles's appearances in Hyde Park drew even larger
crowds; and there was a long debate on the subject in the
correspondence columns of *The Times* and the *Daily Telegraph*,
set in motion by a leg-pulling letter asking if 'this pretty
creature and her pretty ponies' could not somehow be gently
persuaded to go elsewhere because of the delays her presence
caused to persons endeavouring to proceed to and from the
International Exhibition at South Kensington.

The result of the publicity was to end the affair between
Skittles and Harty-Tarty. Skittles established herself as one
of the leading equestrienne-courtesans of Paris, becoming the

mistress of Napoleon III's 63-year old Minister of Finance, Achille Fould. It was while she was in Paris that, in 1863, the young English poet, Wilfred Blunt, fell rapturously in love with her, an experience he treasured for the rest of his long life. When at the end of the 1860s she returned permanently to London, Skittles kept something of a cosy salon at her houses in Mayfair, first in Chesterfield Street and then in South Street. Apart from Blunt, her visitors for Sunday afternoon tea often included the Prince of Wales and Mr Gladstone. In her last years (she died in 1920) she was lame, and the vehicle in which she made excursions in the Park was no longer a phaeton but a bath chair, pushed by an attendant. Among those who paused to salute her courteously as she passed was Lord Kitchener.

Somewhat lower down the scale were the ladies for whom wealthy men provided villas in the outer suburbs and who were visited by their protectors for weekends. Governesses were said to be prone to enticement into this particular kind of love-nest. But for all the attention directed then, and in the second half of the twentieth century, to the seamy side of life in Victorian London, it does seem to have been a time when any Englishman who could afford it would seek the more lurid forms of dissipation in Paris rather than in London.

What presumably struck the foreign visitor to London in the Victorian age was that prostitutes were so plentiful on the streets. Taine was particularly offended by what he called 'the lamentable Haymarket marchpast', since from midday onwards the areas from there to Leicester Square and around Windmill Street were full of heavily-painted women in search of customers. Theatre entrances in general and the Burlington Arcade were also popular hunting grounds. Certain public houses were frequented by reason of their having private rooms. There were numerous accommodation houses, some with the notice 'Beds to Let', and it was to one of these that the majority of women would take their clients. Those who did not get their men from the streets might do so from the 'night houses' such as Kate Hamilton's Café Royal off Leicester Square where assignations could be arranged, the proprietress relying for revenue on the high prices charged for drink.

More popular even than Kate Hamilton's were the Argyll

Rooms in Great Windmill Street which boasted a good
orchestra, brilliant lighting and large gilt mirrors in the main
dance hall and discreet alcoves and subdued lighting in the
gallery, for which an extra charge was made. Mott's in Foley
Street, off Great Portland Street, was very select and kept so
by a hall porter with a gift for letting the gentry and nobility
in and keeping mere rich men out. Other places serving a like
purpose were Laurent's Dancing Academy, also in Windmill
Street, and the Holborn Casino. Brothels as such were illegal,

Highly Respectable Young Persons in Sunday best, 1885

but difficult to suppress; and although some notorious West
End haunts failed to survive the rising site-values and the
street improvements of the 1880s, Booth reported that houses
of accommodation were still in use in the late 1890s and that
the women who plied their trade in such places used the public
lavatories and dressing rooms of central London for painting
their faces before starting their work and for removing this
essential mark of their profession before going home.

The problem of child prostitution was given lurid publicity
in 1885 by the journalistic sensationalism of W. T. Stead of

the *Pall Mall Gazette* who set out to prove that a child could be bought for prostitution abroad, by actually stage-managing the purchase, chloroforming and transfer to Paris of a 13-year old girl whose mother had been paid the sum of £5. He then regaled the readers of the *Pall Mall Gazette* with a highly coloured account of it all, which created a great sensation until it was revealed as a journalist's stunt. Stead and his 2 women agents were given prison sentences for fraudulently removing the child without the parent's consent. Nevertheless, the Criminal Law Amendment Act of 1885, raising the age of consent for a girl from 12 to 16 was rapidly passed largely as a result. Until then it had made little progress; nor could it be denied that child prostitution had existed in the preceding years, partly because little girls and virginity were a cult and partly because fear of venereal disease was universal. One 15-year old informed her (daytime) customer that she was supposed to be at home looking after her 6-year old sister and 8-year old brother while their widowed mother was working as a charwoman. Instead of staying in, she locked the 2 children inside the home and walked along the Strand; the money she obtained from men she spent on meat pies, pastry and sausage rolls. In instantly squandering the money she gained from her sexual activities the child resembled most of the adult members of her profession.

Prostitution at the bottom of the social scale shared to the full the squalor that characterised all other aspects of the lives of the very poor. But, even among the poor, the situation was distorted by the convention that to 'fall' once was to be 'fallen' forever unless 'rescued' by some moral organisation or, (and this was least improbable at the end of the reign) by the Salvation Army. Many women attached themselves to a man out of sheer poverty; out of his own poverty the man might be unable to afford either marriage or any sort of permanent association. The partnership therefore would end and the woman drift off into a profession for which she was entirely unsuited by the mere fact of being so ashamed of having cohabited without the marriage lines of respectability. Women of this sort, the genuine 'unfortunates', were disliked as much by professionals as they were lugubriously bewailed over by middle-class persons with a social conscience.

*Elderly women of the
working class in Lambeth,
1890*

The hardened cases, however, were very hard indeed; Mayhew in the 1850s, Taine in 1872 and the more surgically-minded Charles Booth in the 1890s, were all appalled by what they saw of working-class prostitution. Shadwell, and the whole district by the Ratcliff Highway, made a deep impression on both Mayhew and Taine. The number of the prostitutes, their violence, and their shrill voices, 'like that of a sick owl', convinced Taine that the situation was worse than 'the lowest quarters of Marseilles, Antwerp and Paris; they come nowhere near this'. Mayhew described the women as 'flaunting about bare-headed' in and around the Shadwell public houses, dressed in grubby muslin or cheap blue silk, as having pock-marked faces and, in the case of the more notorious of them, nick-names such as Lushing Loo, Black Sarah and China Emma. They served the physical needs of sailors of every race, colour and creed. The unknown author of *My Secret Life*, however, went on an exploratory visit to the docks with a friend, both in specially selected shabby clothes, without being robbed or being confronted with much more than 'lewd talk' in the various public houses they visited. The fact that this visitor also records that the women were 'without bonnets' indicated how noteworthy this absence of headgear in a woman seemed in Victorian London. It was also recorded that a sailor and a woman who became too noisy as well as rather drunk were forcibly turned out of one public house by the landlord.

135

Further Reading
The works of Taine, Mayhew and Booth already cited
Philip Magnus, *King Edward the Seventh,* 1964
Steven Marcus, *The Other Victorians,* 1966
Henry Blyth, *Skittles, the Last Victorian Courtesan,* 1970
Ronald Pearsall, *The Worm in the Bud,* 1969
E. Beresford Chancellor, *Pleasure Haunts of London,* 1925
Stella Margetson, *Leisure and Pleasure in the 19th Century,* 1969

VII

Hearth and Home

To go much beyond the generalisations and references already made concerning domestic life in London would be difficult and probably misleading. Richard Church, in *Over the Bridge*, for example, wrote of the huggermugger atmosphere of the home life of the masses as tending to make the children 'over-emotional, unadventurous and matriarchal' and it is almost certainly true that as one went down the social scale the family unit became more close and more intimate. Higher up, the household would consist of three separate worlds: of parents; of servants; and of the children, supervised most of the day by nurses or governess or, rather later in the century, by the nanny. Such families would be more patriarchal than those of the lower classes. A major difference separating the richest families from other Londoners would be their habit of living outside the metropolis except during the Season. Another difference would be that respectability and primness would increase the nearer one approached the socially lowest classes. The rich could afford to take the risks of being moderately raffish, since their position was that much more secure; but the lower middle class, and the artisan class indistinguishable from them, felt that they had nothing but their respectability to mark them off from the 'dark, uninstructed masses'. Life in such homes might well be close and comforting; but it could also be suffocating, as the novels of the young H. G. Wells make clear. Hence the contempt for the suburbs expressed both by educated people such as C. F. Masterman, writing in 1909 about a world which was clearly still late-Victorian, and the scorn poured upon it by intellectuals of the Left from the 1880s onwards. In truth, suburban life, neither then nor subsequently, was quite as dreary as the literary-minded have made out; but it bore fairly heavily upon the young all the same, despite their underlying affection for the womb-like surroundings in which they had passed their earliest years.

Throughout the Victorian years, the terrace house slowly declined in social prestige. The style continued on the grand scale only in the West End, and the fashionable inner areas such as Kensington, Bayswater, Mayfair and Belgravia. Sometimes estates of this sort were protected by a gate across the principal access road, with a gatekeeper to keep out hawkers and other undesirables. In less fashionable parts of London, land values were still high enough to make terrace houses normal for those members of the working classes who could afford a small house as well as for middle-class families whose annual income was not above £300 a year (the average family income in the late 1860s in England and Wales has been estimated as about £80 a year). The cheaper the houses, the starker were their exteriors and the more monotonous the appearance of the streets. Social gradation was therefore measured by the degree of ornamentation applied to the facade of a house as well as by its size. The addition of bay windows instantly conferred respectability and if they were decorated by pillars, so much the better. Elaborate porches and door surrounds also conferred status. The next stage up the social scale was the semi-detached villa which, by the last quarter of the century, prevailed wherever in London site values were not so high as to render terrace building economically imperative.

A cosy Victorian interior

The detached villa was only for the most comfortably-off suburban dweller. It was designed to make him feel a measure of kinship with a real country gentleman: like him the villa-dweller had a large garden or even 'grounds' of his own. Villas of the grander sort might be on estates protected, like some of the fashionable inner London developments, by a gate and a gatekeeper, from the intrusion of outsiders. The social pretensions of the occupier of a villa would be further asserted by plentiful use of architectural decoration, with an increasing tendency, as the century proceeded, to Gothic extravagance.

By the end of the century, thanks to the transport revolution, many 'Londoners' were already beginning to live up to 25 miles (40 km) from the centre. Others among the better off would have permanent residences or 'cottages' built in Kent or Surrey. Here, the architectural styles of Norman Shaw and Philip Webb allied to the horticultural skills of Gertrude Jekyll started a whole new fashion in home- and garden-making that was to spread downwards through the classes in all parts of outer suburbia during the succeeding half-century. Another innovation in late Victorian times which brought a change in the character of the home life of the many who now travelled in from the suburbs for work or pleasure was the increased use of cafés and restaurants. The humbler as well as the better-paid office workers might resort to them for a midday meal; there were cheap restaurants like Lockhart's chain or grand ones like the Holborn Restaurant. Lady shoppers could recover from their exertions by taking tea in teashops if they did not use the restaurants which the departmental stores provided for them; and visits to the theatre would be preceded by a restaurant meal. Similarly, the increased number of hotels, including such large ones as the Langham, the Piccadilly and the Hotel Russell catered for the many who were precluded by the expense and their all-male exclusiveness from membership of the London clubs. In these various ways, for the better off at least, something of the all-inclusive self-sufficiency of home life had diminished by the end of the Victorian age.

For the majority of those who lived and worked in the metro-polis, however, the ideal to be aspired to was that of the home as a cosy, comfortable and harmonious retreat within which the harsh realities of a competitive and sinful metropolitan world could be totally forgotten. Inevitably, as a larger proportion of the population could afford to spend money upon their homes, there was decline in taste and by the 1850s domestic interiors became excessively cluttered with bric-à-brac of all sorts, with a particular tendency towards the end of the reign for oriental embellishments: brass tables, Japanese fans, Indian rugs and carpets and the aspidistra became fashionable.

By contrast, neither bathroom nor waterclosets were universal middle-class domestic phenomena and until the 1850s the principal source of illumination was either the candle or the oil lamp. The use of gaslighting did not extend from the middle to the lower classes until the introduction of slot meters in the last decade of the reign; the gas cooker by that time was also coming into general use. But the padded sofas, plush armchairs, embroidered boxes and baskets and footstools, stuffed birds and potted plants, could all nevertheless testify to the lavish and loving care which the home inspired in the Victorians. Nowhere more than in the metropolis can the home have provided so needful an assertion of the primacy of human values against those of the office, the shop and the factory; and even if the taste was bad, the feelings it expressed were almost certainly genuine.

In larger houses, the rooms would be functional. The morning room was for breakfast, the schoolroom for the older children and their governess, the nursery for the younger children and their nurse, the dining room for eating in, often heavily furnished and solemnised with dark crimson wallpaper, and the drawing room in which to receive calls and spend the evening. This necessitated the provision of a piano. Most houses with any pretensions would also have a conservatory; only very large ones would have a billiard room and a library. Smoking constituted something of a problem, since cigars were the manly smoke for men, though even ladies were prepared to smoke cigarettes in the privacy of their own home at the end of the century. Queen Victoria smoked cigarettes on picnics 'to keep the flies away'. Gentlemen were given to wearing corduroy or velvet smoking jackets and sometimes a smoking cap, often shaped like a Turkish fez, complete with tassel. This was to prevent the hair and clothes from being permeated by the odour of the tobacco. The lower orders had to be content

with a kitchen and a parlour, or perhaps a back room and a front room, the latter being a 'best' room, more often cleaned and dusted than actually used. For the rest, the very lowest class continued to live in general squalor, in Tennyson's words, 'hovelled and hustled together, each sex, like swine'.

Almost every Victorian family that considered itself socially respectable proclaimed its status by employing as many servants as its finances could stand. At the very least, a daily girl or one girl living-in, was essential if the lady of the house was to avoid demeaning herself by engaging in domestic manual labour. The purely Victorian notion that women, if they were ladies, should have no real occupation was particularly strong in the better-off parts of London, where there would be few opportunities to display old-fashioned feminine skills such as making wine or bread and where the temptation to ape the behaviour of the very rich would be so much stronger than elsewhere. It degraded the husband as well as the wife if she worked about the house and, just as, ideally, a gentleman was someone who did not work at all or, if he did, relied chiefly on an income from land and investments rather than on a salary; so, ideally, a lady was one who did not do anything at all except display her 'accomplishments', or engage in intermittent good works among the poor. Hence the emphasis on embroidery, water-colouring, singing and piano-playing and hence, too, the demand for 'polite' literature suitable for reading aloud in drawing rooms in the long winter evenings. There also developed in the Victorian period the comforting idea that if a lady engaged in household work she was failing in her duty to provide employment to the labouring classes. Society developed its own 'who does what' system. Domestic work was strictly for the domestics and it was crossing an economic as well as a social demarcation line for a lady to poach on the working-class 'right' to earn its living by carrying buckets of coal and jugs of hot water up three or four flights of stairs and to clean the rooms before breakfast. Gwen Raverat's admittedly eccentric aunt, who had never in her life posted a letter or put a piece of coal on the fire and who regarded herself as worked to death if in the absence of a domestic she was compelled to answer her own doorbell, was not altogether unrepresentative of the ideal Victorian lady.

The gap between employers and servants tended to widen in Victorian times. This was partly to reassure those whose social status was newly attained that they really had arrived. No servant, it was laid down, should ever sit in the presence of her employers, never express an opinion uninvited and never, save as a response to such a greeting from an employer, say 'Good morning' or 'Good evening'.

One kept as many servants as one could afford. The gloomy young man in Tennyson's poem, *Maud*, who thought himself very hard done-by, declared, 'I am nameless and poor' and immediately sought to confirm the fact by saying, 'I keep but a man and a maid' adding too, that they were 'ever ready to slander and steal'. Indeed, as the Victorian period went on, it became increasingly hard to get reliable servants. Although about 1 in every 15 employed persons in London was a domestic servant, rising middle-class standards meant that demand constantly exceeded supply. The wealthiest households, perhaps employing house steward, butler, housekeeper, cook, ladies' maid, head nurse, nursemaid, gardener, footmen, page boys and stable boys, with many other lowly-paid domestics to assist them, probably still managed to get along, because there was a cachet in serving in such households, much chance of obtaining perquisites from tradesmen or otherwise cheating their employer, as well as the chance to find a husband or a wife from among the other staff. At best there was, for the women, a chance of acquiring some training in the arts of domestic management which might prove the foundation of a decent married life, even if there was also the chance of being 'ruined' by the attentions of one of the young masters of the house. The loneliness and drudgery of being the one maid-of-all-work or even one of only two or three young servants in a smaller suburban household did at least have the compensating factors of a safe, if not comfortable, lodging, and free regular

*emi-detached villas in Balham,
nsidered as a good example of
1odern architecture' in 1870*

meals. The average wage for girls throughout the United Kingdom in 1867 was reckoned to be 7s 10d (39p) a week or just over £20 a year; thus, a servant girl earning between £14 and £18 a year in London as a domestic servant was, by the low standards of the time, slightly better off than the average working girl and certainly better off than the average male under 20, whose average weekly pay was thought to be 7s 3d (36p) a week, or £18.75 a year.

Middle-class home life in Victorian London was, by the overriding conventions of the age, inward-looking to an exceptional degree. It is therefore all the more valuable if it becomes possible to turn to the particular rather than to rely solely on generalities. The recorded events of one obscure middle-class London household for the year 1883, which have accidentally survived, may serve to illustrate some of the preoccupations and problems of the private lives of this section of society. The record is that of a diarist reporting events in his own household and should serve as a reminder that any one household would in general conform to the standard stereotype, but in particulars would also deviate from it.

The head of the household in question was a retired army surgeon from a Highland regiment, living in a rented terrace house in Ledbury Road, Bayswater. He had retired from the army in 1867, after service in the Crimea and the Indian

Mutiny. He had married in 1873. Not only was his wife, Harriet, 26 years his junior; she was socially 'beneath' him, her birth certificate indicating that she was the daughter of an Oxfordshire farm labourer. When her future husband first met her she appears to have been installed in a tobacconist's shop in Peckham, a device often used by young women who wished, for whatever reason, to serve a male clientèle. She had by the time of her marriage already had two children, the father of the second of them being her future husband; both children had died in infancy.

At the time of their marriage Harriet was again pregnant and her husband appears to have entered upon the marriage principally to make an honest man of himself, since he had recorded his growing unease at living in what he inaccurately called 'adultery'. He was very conscious of having broken the social code by marrying Harriet and it was a full year before he felt brave enough to make the fact of his marriage known to his friends and relations. Notwithstanding, he remained a dutiful churchgoer, regularly attending Sunday morning service at St Peter's, Bayswater.

He remained a member of the Junior United Service Club after his marriage. He sometimes dined there, but more usually seems to have gone there after dining at home round about 6·30 or sometimes earlier. He carefully notes the deaths of fellow officers, particularly those of the rank of lieutenant-colonel and above. The size of his army pension and of such private income as he had is not known. He used omnibuses and the underground railway frequently, but cabs only rarely. When called to Edinburgh to his brother-in-law's funeral, he makes a point of noting that he travelled second class, doubtless because, since he was not a servant but was undoubtedly a gentleman, he ought to have gone first class. He bought his coal at Whiteley's at 25s (£1.25) a ton and husbanded it with Victorian thrift. On 3 Jan 1883, he wrote, 'We resumed the fire in the back dining room which we have not had for a week, the weather was so warm'; on 3 November, he reports with apparent pride, 'only began fire in the dining room today. Most people began fires weeks ago.'

By the beginning of 1883 his family consisted of his eldest daughter, who was 10 in the February, another daughter aged 4 and a boy of 3; and Harriet was 2 or 3 months into the eighth of her 9 recorded pregnancies. Apart from the 2 children who had died before her marriage, 2 others had also died in infancy after marriage, but she eventually had 5 children who survived into adult life. From time to time the diarist reports going with his two younger children to Kensington Gardens where he 'played' or 'ran about' with them. He also bought them a rocking horse. It was a secondhand one and cost him £1 4s (£1.20). The elder daughter, Frances, was boarded at a school in Ladbroke Grove kept by a Mrs Bosworth.

The outside activities and interests of the head of the household were modestly representative of those of his social betters, but tinged with a certain scholarly curiosity. He had a Victorian liking for puns and was to contribute a rather bad one to the correspondence columns of the *Pall Mall Gazette* in 1902. He was devoted to the close daily reading of the strongly Conservative *St James's Gazette*. He kept a commonplace book, but added nothing to it in 1883. In 1882 he had copied from the *Sporting Times* a paragraph about Lady Sarah Lennox because 'I knew the eminently handsome, courteous General Sir William Napier, her son, author of *The History of the Peninsular War*, who had, too, some beautiful daughters.' At other times he interests himself in small linguistic exactitudes: '*Coute que coute* is right; not *coute qui coute* as is generally said in England', he notes on one occasion. On another, he records that there is some doubt whether it was true that in *Les Travailleurs de la Mer* Victor Hugo called the Firth of Forth *La Première de la Quatrième* but rather that he wrote of '*la falaise Premier des Quatres*'. One entry in the book, however, is completely relevant to Victorian domestic life in general as well as to his own. He writes:

> *The Coffin by the Cradle:*
> Told the struggle that was o'er
> Hope whispered in the Mother's ear
> 'Tis but an angel more!'

Mrs Lacey our neighbour sent these lines to us on death of our little infant boy who died after fearful suffering on August 29th 1875 at Ramsgate.

During 1883, however, most of his time is taken up, in characteristic Victorian fashion, with writing and receiving letters and paying and receiving calls. Perhaps because the air of the metropolis was still under suspicion because of its dampness and smoke-engendered fogs and of the persistence of miasmatist theories about the transmission of disease, he was obsessed with meteorological conditions; or this may merely have been one example of the Victorian passion for facts for their own sake, especially 'scientific' ones. Whatever else was recorded, and even if there was nothing else to note, the day's weather was always faithfully reported. 'A sort of mist', he writes on 21 January, 'which keeps the streets filthy' and the theme of dirty streets appears again at the year's end.

He would clearly not tolerate shortcomings in the transport system of the metropolis. On 3 June he got on a Metropolitan train at Westbourne Park to travel to see his widowed sister and her daughter at Richmond. '14 in compartment. Got out at Notting Hill [now Ladbroke Grove station] and walked back to Westbourne Park, to get money back. Clerk refused.' On the following day, *en route* to his Club, he 'looked in at Metropolitan Ry office to complain at not getting a place after paying for ticket'. Eight days later the Metropolitan manager wrote to him enclosing stamps to the value of 1s 4d (6½p) by way of repayment. On 2 August, in addition to buying a pair of 'boots (gaiter)' at Kelsey's, Victoria, for 21 shillings (£1.05) he wrote to the secretary of the London General Omnibus Company reporting a 'cad' (conductor) for insolence; but there is no record that the 'General' was as handsomely forthcoming as the Metropolitan.

Apart from occasional shopping expeditions, a few trips to Hyde Park and Kensington Gardens and the Sunday church-going, husband and wife appear to have done little together outside the home. Partly this was a consequence of her condition: their baby was born in the first week of July. By 13 April, 'Harriet thinks she is too unsightly to pay visits' and for that reason he called on the new vicar of St Peter's (the Rev Mr Oldham) and Mrs Oldham, and left a card for his wife and '2 of my own'. They evidently understood the complicated ritual of how many visiting cards to leave at a house when they called; and apparently when not approaching or recovering

from one of her pregnancies, Harriet conformed to the other
ritual of setting aside a day of the week on which to be 'at
home' to visitors. It was on account of one of their frequent
crises over the servants that on 16 November the diarist 'wrote
(for H) a note apologising for her not being in on her reception
day (Wednesday)'. Visits to places of entertainment were
rare. On 18 January he and his wife and niece went 'to the
Piccadilly Hall and saw Chang the Giant (whom I had seen
before, in 1866) 8 ft 4 [284 cm]'. On a Saturday evening in
October his wife 'with servant Mary' went to 'a theatre,
Ladbroke Hill [Hall?] in evening'.

He evidently shared the Victorian Londoner's liking for
exhibitions. A Fisheries Exhibition was held at South Kensington that year. He reports its opening by the Prince of Wales
on 12 May, visited it on 12 June, declaring himself 'pleased',
went a second time on 14 August and 4 days later went a
third time, taking his wife and daughter with him. He also
describes as a 'very enjoyable excursion' a walk through
Bushey Park followed by an inspection of 'the pictures at
Hampton Court' in the company of his sister, her daughter
and three other unmarried ladies, in June. Often, like his
social superiors, he was to be seen in Hyde Park in fine weather
making his way to his Club in St James's. He went to the Royal
Academy in February to an 'Exhibition of Old Masters.
Pleased'. On 27 June he went 'to Lord's by bus, hoping to
see Oxford v Cambs match, being the 3rd day: found it was
just over. Cambs won.'

He went to his club, on average, about twice a week, made
regular trips by bus or rail to the Pay Office to collect his
pension, and attended lectures at the Royal United Services
Institute. On 9 May there was a discussion there at which both
Lord Chelmsford and Lord Wolseley 'spoke well'; and he
heard a paper read, on 22 June, by 'Surgeon-Major de Chau-
mont, on Military Hygiene'. His regiment continued to
command his affection. On 31 May he attended its annual
'dinner at Willis's – present, about 76. Duke of Albany, etc'.
The highlight of his social life in 1883 came on 7 March when
he dined as 'Col Britten's guest at Clothworkers' Hall. Prince
Teck, D of Leeds, Lord Wolseley &c there and Mr Forster—
many speeches. A Miss —— drove Britten and Mrs and me

home in her carriage in a snowstorm: bitterly cold'. He had shown a certain anxiety about this function, writing on 28 February 'to Mansion House by rail to explore for Mincing Lane where I am to dine with Lt-Col Britten. He came after dinner with a card of invitation to Clothworkers' Dinner'. It is interesting that, though doubtless dressed appropriately for this important occasion, he travelled to it by the underground; his return journey in a private carriage is the only occasion that year on which he appears to have travelled in such a vehicle.

His other principal activity during the year was to concern himself about the widows of two fellow officers. Indeed, the number of widows with single daughters he visited and corresponded with was high; one widowed lady sent him snowdrops from the country in the spring and roses in the summer. On 23 January, a Mrs Rudyard visited him. She 'seems in difficulties—pecuniary'. On the 25th she wrote saying she was *destitute*. Very sad'. Promptly, he went to his Club and secured £5 for her 'from Lt-Col Read: went to her and gave it to her, with £5 of *my own*'. On the following day, it being the occasion of the Club's annual general meeting, he collected another '2 sovns' for Mrs Rudyard. The case of Mrs Edgar was more intractable. Her husband died on 28 March and the diarist, 'greatly shocked and grieved', spent from then until October trying to raise money for Mrs Edgar. He wrote to the regiment, to the Chelsea Hospital and to an organisation called the Patriotic Fund on her behalf, almost to no avail. Since earlier diaries kept in the 1860s also contain frequent references to appeals made to him for cash or loans or guarantees from acquaintances in financial difficulty, one gets from these records a sense of how insecure was the prosperity of these lesser members of the middle class, particularly officers' widows and the junior officers who frequented the London Clubs.

It was doubtless Harriet's pregnancy that accounted for the presence in the household of her mother for the greater part of the year; she was there for a month in the winter and again in the spring and from early May till late August ('*16 weeks here*', the diarist italicises). Save for a reference to her abandonment of visits in mid-April there are few references to Harriet's own

condition. In early May she gave up going to church; in early
June she was taken out in a bath chair; on 20 June she was
'poorly'. On 5 July, the diarist writes as follows:

> Fine weather. On coming down this morning at 9 found
> that H had been in labour almost all night: doctor sent
> for at 5 a.m. Labour slow: he had gone home to breakfast
> &c. We sent for him again; the child, large, dark-haired
> born at 10.30. Telegraphed to sister Mary: pcards to
> Mrs Connor [whose ill-health had caused him to visit her
> several times that month]; to Mrs Rudyard [for whom
> he was still writing in vain to the Patriotic Fund]; to
> sister Anne in Edinburgh; wrote note to Mrs Bosworth for
> Fanny's benefit; sent advertisement to *The Times* with
> 6s payable to Geo Edw Wright.

Nine days later, the baby was 'fractious, causing us uneasiness.
A *dose of castor oil* did good'. Twenty-four days after the birth,
however, Harriet was taken out, the weather being fine, in a
bath chair, with her husband and Fanny in attendance. By
3 August he is writing, 'Fine. Out shopping with H *she walking*
— 1st time since baby was born'. On 15 August they went
shopping in Westbourne Grove but, owing to a heavy storm
he took his wife home by cab. On 23 August sufficient progress
had been made for Harriet's mother to end her 16-week stay;
but complications immediately followed. The 3-year old boy
and 4-year old girl both had diarrhoea, due, the father
considered, to their having eaten 'many grapes yesterday and
swallowing the skins'. As a result Harriet was 'very seedy'
and two days later, though the other children were better,
'That baby, H thinks, will not live. Certainly his face looks
almost dropsical and pasty'. In view of her previous experiences,
the departure of her mother and the 'uselessness of the servants',
Harriet's fears are understandable. Fortunately, by the end
of the day, 'Baby looks much better this evening' and thereafter
the only references to him relate to his baptism at St Peter's,
Bayswater, by the Rev Mr Oldham, and to the problem of his
vaccination. The vigilance of the public health authorities was
already well established in this connection and promptly on
the day the baby was 3 months old, an enquiry from the local
vaccination officer was received as to why the child had not

been vaccinated. Despite suffering from diarrhoea after eating roast goose ('never had so severe dysentry before', he writes, which, given his years of service in West Africa, North America, the Crimea and India, is remarkable) he did the vaccinating himself. It did not take; and the diarist had another attack of diarrhoea, which he blamed on the soup. A week later he failed again and went 'to the Local Govt Board for more vacc lymph'. This time, 'vaccinated baby with lymph in tube from Local Govt Board *with success*: very satisfactory'. A certificate was duly 'sent to the Vacc Office'.

That from time to time the food served in the house should have upset his stomach is hardly surprising, given the ample evidence the diary provides of the chaotic situation created by the problem of finding and keeping suitable servants. Indeed, to judge from the record, the recruitment of domestic staff was the greatest single preoccupation of the year. Apart from frequent visits in search of suitable girls, time was taken up in writing for, or providing, references for servants. The total wages bill on domestic service for the year was £24 7s 4d (£24.37), a figure, according to Mrs Beeton, appropriate to a household income of perhaps just above £300 a year but certainly well below £500. Harriet probably did much of her own cooking.

The family began the year with two servants, Mary Daylor and Annie Timms, the latter being the nursemaid. Both were paid 16s 8d (83p) a month, a yearly rate of £10. Annie left on 21 March. The diarist's accounts record reads:

> Annie Timms pd to 21 March 16 8
> and left. I pd her fare home 7 4
> (like a fool).

Mrs Beeton's arrangement of a table, with floral decoration, suitable for a dinner party for twelve persons

Annie was replaced by Ellen Leary, engaged at only £8 a year. At the end of April, Mary Daylor also left, her work apparently being unsatisfactory. She failed to answer the door to the new Vicar of St Peter's and his wife when the diarist and Harriet were out. Her replacement, Catherine Nestor, came at £8 a year, raised to £9 in August. Ellen Leary lasted only until 15 May, when she was paid 11s 6d (57½p) having earned, since her arrival on 21 March, a total of 24s 10d (£1.24). Two days later, 'Ellen Leary's Mother (& Aunt) came crying bitterly when told her daughter had left. I gave her the address and I wrote to EL telling her to write to her mother at once and to us'. Impatiently, he wrote only two days afterwards, 'Surprised not to hear from Ellen Leary to whom I sent a stamped envelope'; but before the day was out he noted, accompanying the sentence with the two crosses he used to denote important events like deaths and births, 'Glad to get a letter at last from Ellen Leary saying she is all right'.

From March to June they were preoccupied with trying to get a third servant. Harriet went all the way to Stamford Hill on 3 March to try to get a certain 'Julia Tuckwell to come back'; on 10 March husband and wife 'went to St Elizabeth Home and saw Sister Aloysius about a servant. A girl Maggy Welsh, was sent afterwards but 'we fear she is in bad health and won't do'. St Elizabeth's was a home for children attached to a Franciscan convent opened in the Portobello Road in 1862. In April, relief was forthcoming: 'a note from Julia Tuckwell's sister Emmie, saying she will come to us'. Emmie was paid as much as £16 a year and perhaps this explains why the accounts describe her as 'Miss Tuckwell'. Four days after Harriet's confinement she left; it may be that she had been engaged solely for that particular period.

Meanwhile, they had not done with Mary Daylor. At the beginning of May, Mary wrote 'expressing regret for short-comings whilst here and asking to come back'. On 30 May she was re-engaged at her previous wage of £10 a year. She was given notice again on 16 July, but was saved either by Harriet's inability so soon after her confinement to start looking for another servant or by the simultaneous departure of 'Miss Tuckwell'. In August, Mary was again told to get another place and again reprieved. She was finally dismissed on 22

December, though the master of the house paid her the full
16s 8d (83p) for the month and commented, 'Poor little Mary
Daylor left—cruel—went to lodgings—no chance of getting
a place at this Xmas time'.

Reduced as she had been by the end of August to the services
of the unreliable Mary Daylor and the unremarkable Catherine
Nestor, Harriet was soon in dire straits. 'H worked to death,'
the diary records, 'servants useless'. Three girls failed in quick
succession to give satisfaction as nursemaids. One 'could not
rise before 7' and another 'took away 4 aprons not hers and
stole Mary Daylor's purse with money in it, 8s [40p] odd'.
That these mischances appeared in no way out of the ordinary
seems to be confirmed by the diarist's view on 31 December
that the year had been 'almost a blank'.

Further Reading
(None of the following is specifically about domestic life in Victorian
London, though containing references to it. The material for the
second half of this chapter is in unpublished papers in the possession
of the author)
Marion Lochheed, *The Victorian Household*, 1964
Dorothy Marshall, *The English Domestic Servant in History*, 1949
John Gloag, *Victorian Comfort*, 1961 and *Victorian Taste*, 1962
Gillian Avery, *Victorian People*, 1970
E. S. Turner, *What the Butler Saw*, 1962

VIII

Theatre and Music Hall

It was only in the early Victorian period that the London theatre finally gained its freedom from the restrictive policy of the eighteenth-century licensing acts which among other things had sought to prevent the performance of stage plays outside the City of Westminster and to limit performances to the two 'patent' theatres at Drury Lane and Covent Garden. For these regulations, the Theatres Act, 1843, substituted the rule that the Lord Chamberlain should withhold his licence for a play only 'in the interest of good manners, decorum or the public peace'. This enabled the drama to enjoy that freedom from government restriction that was currently being extended in the world of commerce to imports and exports; and it expanded accordingly. But as late as 1879 Matthew Arnold asserted with some truth that there was 'no English theatre' and later still Bernard Shaw was to say much the same thing more frequently and more pungently. What they both meant was that the London theatre provided for the most part melodramatic or spectacular entertainment. The classic repertoire of English drama was to a considerable extent neglected, partly because the seventeenth-century dramatists were considered licentious and the few eighteenth-century ones were considered artificial. Shakespeare was represented by only a limited choice from the canon and for long his texts were butchered or offered in various revised forms, in both cases to provide time for scenic extras. The broad taste, long-surviving, was for heavy melodrama, often based on Victorian novels, such as Mrs Henry Wood's *East Lynne* and Dickens' *Christmas Carol,* of which there were four presentations in

Leicester Square, circa *1875*

London in 1844, after which it was performed almost every Christmas. As an alternative, there were farces in plenty, most of them adapted from the French. At least until the 1870s, the dominant personality in a theatre was either the manager or more usually the actor, hardly ever the playwright. Even at the end of the century, despite the emergence of Henry Arthur Jones and Arthur Wing Pinero, the brief iridescence of Oscar Wilde, the faint shadow cast by Ibsen and the largely ignored imprecations of Bernard Shaw, London still provided an actor's or an actor-manager's theatre.

The 5 dominant playhouses of the Victorian era were the Theatre Royal, Drury Lane, Her Majesty's Theatre in the Haymarket, the Theatre Royal, Haymarket (usually referred to simply as the Haymarket), the Royal Opera House, Covent Garden and (at intervals) the Lyceum. From the end of 1841 until 1843, Drury Lane was managed by the actor, William Charles Macready, who did much to bring prestige to the theatre and to begin the slow process, which took almost the whole of the reign, of raising the tone of theatre-going. It was considered a striking novelty that, under Macready, the seats in the pit were covered with handsome red cloth, that each person had a separate stall and that there was a central gangway. Macready also drove the women of pleasure from the purlieus of Drury Lane; and a state visit to the theatre by Queen Victoria and Prince Albert in 1843 was one of the few marks of royal favour bestowed upon the theatre in Victorian times until the 1880s. Macready presented and acted in *The Merchant of Venice, Henry V* and *Macbeth,* but lost money in the process; and after various changes of management Drury Lane became famous chiefly for spectacular plays and for its annual pantomimes. From 1880 onwards it contrived to introduce into its plays such wonders as one ship exploding and another sinking, a midnight snowstorm in Piccadilly Circus, undersea divers, steam yachts passing through Boulter's Lock and a representation of the scene at Rorke's Drift in the Zulu War.

Until the 1850s, Her Majesty's was notable chiefly for opera and ballet and for audiences said to be the most brilliantly fashionable in Europe. It was here that the 'Swedish nightingale', Jenny Lind, made her London debut in 1847, and where *Fidelio* was first performed in England in 1851. Burned to the ground in 1867 (most of the more historic theatres in London seem to have been as vulnerable to fire as the early music halls) it was rebuilt in 1868–69 but not used again as a theatre until in 1877 it re-opened as an opera house with Bellini's *Norma*. Demolished in 1890, it was re-opened after that on only a small part of the original site—which had formerly extended as far south as to include the site of the modern New Zealand House—by Henry Beerbohm Tree. Tree built it out of the profit he had made at the Haymarket theatre on the opposite side of the road with an adaptation of Charles Du Maurier's novel *Trilby*. From then on into Edward VII's reign, Tree put on a number of highly spectacular Shakespearian productions.

The Theatre Royal, Haymarket, had its exterior designed by John Nash, although its interior was twice reconstructed, and was managed from 1837 to 1853 by Benjamin Webster. It was among the first theatres to cut off that part of the stage which had normally protruded in front of the curtain and had been flanked by side boxes whose occupants were thus in close proximity to the actors. Webster thereby moved the orchestra nearer to the actors and used the space thus vacated to create 'orchestra stalls' in front of the pit.

The Royal Opera House, Covent Garden had begun life in 1732 as the Theatre Royal, Covent Garden. During the first three Victorian decades it was managed as a theatre under Macready until 1839 and Charles Mathews until 1842 but, after a period during which it was used as a London headquarters by the Anti-Corn Law League, its interior was redesigned in 1847 and it was re-opened as the Royal Italian Opera House, Covent Garden, with a performance of Rossini's *Semiramide*. Thus, though significant in, and often synonymous with, the history of opera in England, it contributed little to the Victorian theatre.

The Royal Italian Opera House, Covent Garden, 1855:
The Queen and Prince Albert with Napoleon III and the
Empress Eugénie

Mr and Mrs Charles Kean in Macbeth,
circa *1858*

The most important name in the London theatre of the 1850s was Charles Kean, who, with his wife, produced a number of Shakespearian revivals, as well as many melodramas, at the Princess's Theatre on the north side of Oxford Street. Kean's productions were spectacular in the extreme and therefore much admired; he was the Queen's favourite actor. He employed outstandingly skilful scene painters and at times used moving dioramas as a background. Like most Victorian managers he was much given to the use of transparent gauzes to suggest visions or actions taking place in a dream; and to the clever use of trapdoors. The meticulousness of the scene-painting for Kean's Shakespearian productions included particular attention to precise topographical detail. Since *The Merchant of Venice* was for the most part set in Venice, the most elaborate care was taken to ensure that the stage looked as much like Venice as possible, even if the words spoken by the actors were often not those, or rarely all of those, actually accredited to Shakespeare. Kean thus offered a careful blending of some Shakespeare with a great deal of spectacle, much sentiment, a deal of irrelevant, if painstaking scholarship (a common Victorian phenomenon) together with as many balletic extras as the mutilated text could be made to accommodate. The result was highly effective entertainment and Kean succeeded in carrying on Macready's short-lived tradition of bringing elegant society back into the theatre. It was, indeed, in his time that the London theatre at last began to become respectable. There were orderly box office arrangements for the first time and it began to be mandatory to wear evening dress in the stalls.

156

The brief early Victorian revival of Sadler's Wells in Finsbury, under Samuel Phelps, was a consequence of the legislation which made it possible for Shakespeare's plays to be presented elsewhere than in Westminster. Sadler's Wells had had two centuries of fairly disorderly history and it was an achievement on Phelps's part to put on 34 of Shakespeare's plays between 1844 and 1862; by the latter date Phelps had given altogether over 3,000 performances and one or two of Shakespeare's plays were presented by him that had not been seen on the stage for a couple of centuries. Phelps had no successors who were worthy of him. Sadler's Wells was used variously during the latter half of the Victorian period as a skating rink, a pickle factory, a purveyor of the crudest melodrama to very rough audiences and, by 1893, as a music hall. By 1906, after serving for a time as a cinema, it was derelict until re-opening in 1931 under Lilian Baylis, who made it once more a major influence in the London theatre.

Another theatre of importance was on the site occupied in the twentieth century by the Scala Theatre in Charlotte Street. It had a variety of names and fortunes and in early Victorian times was considered 'the lowest theatre in London'. In 1865, it was renovated and renamed the Prince of Wales' Theatre and produced the next major change in the character of the London stage after the reigns of Macready at Drury Lane and Kean at the Princess's. For most of the period from 1865 to 1880, The Prince of Wales' was under the management of the Bancrofts: Marie Wilton and her husband and leading man, Squire Bancroft. The Bancrofts and their principal dramatist, Tom Robertson, introduced a welcome note of naturalism into their productions, the most notable in this respect being *Society* (1866) and *Caste* (1867). Although the result was seen later in the century merely as the replacement of melodrama by a somewhat simpering gentility, the Bancrofts, like Kean in his day, were successful in raising the tone of the theatre in keeping with the improvement in manners in general. In the 1880s, the Bancrofts moved to the Haymarket.

A new theatre in Coventry Street which had opened in 1884, took over the name of Prince of Wales' when the original theatre of that name closed in 1886, and was memorable for its presentation of the famous and often-revived farce, *The*

A Gaiety Girl *poster by Douglas Hardy, 1895*

Private Secretary, by Charles Hawtrey, which eventually ran for 785 performances and earned him a profit of £100,000. The second Prince of Wales' was also the starting point of the musical comedy as an entertainment form, the first two presentations in this genre being *In Town* (1892) which was afterwards transferred to the Gaiety, and *A Gaiety Girl* (1893). The Prince of Wales' also presented the play called *The Only Way* which was based on Dickens's *Tale of Two Cities*. With Martin Harvey in the role of Sidney Carton, it remained a favourite with less-sophisticated audiences well into the twentieth century.

When the Bancrofts took over the Haymarket they had it re-designed to provide for the first time a picture-frame stage with a proscenium on all four sides. This complete separation of actors from spectators was thus a relatively modern development in the theatre; and it sorted well with the determination of the Bancrofts to make their profession appear glamorously elegant and apart. Their new interior was attractively up-holstered, the stage was always attractively set and the prices tended to be on the high side. By the 1880s, the practice of charging half a guinea ($52\frac{1}{2}$p) for a seat in the stalls was well established and ensured that only the better off could afford good seats in the theatres of the West End. The poorer sort were confined to 'the gods', as the top gallery was called, and it was not until about this period that the practice of queuing for the gallery was substituted for what had hitherto been a free-for-all. The Bancrofts were so successful that they enjoyed the personal patronage of the Prince of Wales, a circumstance which enabled him to suggest that they allow his friend Lily Langtry to make her stage début as the leading lady in a charity performance of *She Stoops to Conquer* given at the Haymarket in 1881 before what *The Times* called 'the most distinguished audience ever seen in a theatre'. Mrs Langtry was well and truly launched, taking the lead in a production of Tom Robertson's comedy about the Crimean War called *Ours* in 1882. The Prince was so delighted with what the Bancrofts had done for 'the Jersey Lily', who subsequently had a successful stage career on both sides of the Atlantic, that he gave a much publicised dinner at Marlborough House that year to which, among other stage celebrities, he invited Bancroft, George Grossmith, Henry Irving, John Hare and William Kendal. At least one of the aristocratic guests also invited thought the occasion 'dullish'. The closest association the younger members of the aristocracy had with the theatrical profession was probably the result of the attractions of the young ladies who appeared in the musical comedies at the Gaiety Theatre in the 1890s.

It was Irving who carried on from the Bancrofts the process of elevating the standing of the theatrical profession, but he did so without adding anything significant to English drama except his own skill in turning into moving tragedy material which lesser actors could hardly have raised above the level of hack melodrama. There is a very real sense in which Irving was like the best music hall performers of the time in that, like them, he could transform often intrinsically poor material by the sheer power of a vibrantly projected personality. He was certainly not without contacts with the world of the music hall. A story is told of a conversation he had with Harry Hart, at one time owner of the Bedford Music Hall. Hart asked Irving how business was at the Lyceum and received the reply, 'Not too flourishing, I fear; most of my patrons seem to be going to the Opera. And how are things with you?' Hart's reply was, 'Terrible, Sir 'Enry. All my customers have gone 'opping'. Irving was as acceptable to the social class that also enjoyed opera as the music hall stars were to working-class Londoners whose only chance of a holiday was the opportunity to spend a fortnight at the end of the summer working in the Kentish hopfields; though some of the material Irving worked with would hardly have been out of place in the music hall. This certainly applies to his celebrated performance as Mathias in *The Bells* (adapted as usual from the French). But Irving got his knighthood in 1895 (and honorary degrees from Dublin, Cambridge and Glasgow) for a personal dignity and a superb versatility that were without precedent in the English theatre. Better still from the point of view of the profession, his knighthood was a precedent from which Squire Bancroft, George Alexander (manager and actor at the St James's) and Beerbohm Tree all benefited; the last-named when about to receive the accolade, was so nervous that he is reported to have asked if he could 'have it with gas'.

Ellen Terry played most of the leading female roles in Shakespeare either with or without Irving in a long stage career, being acclaimed in particular for her portrayal of Ophelia. It is doubtful if any actress was ever more universally admired. Among her qualities she was said, by sober judges, to possess an enchanting personality, a fine aesthetic sense and the capacity of investing everything she did with charm. She survived to appear in some of Shaw's plays in the Edwardian period and to live to the age of 80, dying, still surrounded with an aura of adoration, in 1928.

Smartness and distinction were characteristic of (Sir)

Romeo and Juliet *at the Lyceum, with Irving as Romeo*

George Alexander's gentlemanly acting and smooth production in the society dramas written in the 1890s by (Sir) Arthur
Pinero. The appearance of Mrs Patrick Campbell in Pinero's
The Second Mrs Tanqueray in 1893 was a sensation so great that
the play and her performance were both remembered for a
generation as positively 'daring'. The emergence of the
formidable 'Mrs Pat' as a native-born actress of force to
compete with the overpowering French actresses, Sarah
Bernhardt and Eleanora Duse, further illustrates that the
Victorian theatre was above all a vehicle for actors and
actresses, as for set designers and scene painters.

No account of theatrical entertainment in Victorian London
can ignore the extraordinary phenomenon of Gilbert and
Sullivan. Rupert D'Oyly Carte had first produced *Trial by
Jury* by these celebrated collaborators at the Royalty Theatre
in Dean Street, Soho and as a result had formed a Comedy
Opera Company which staged *The Sorcerer*, *H.M.S. Pinafore*,
and *The Pirates of Penzance* between 1877 and 1881. In the latter
year, D'Oyly Carte opened the Savoy Theatre in the Strand
with a transfer of *Patience*, its opening night at the theatre
being a glittering affair, with an audience such as might have
been seen at Covent Garden itself. From then until 1893, the
Savoy was a permanent home for Gilbert and Sullivan operas,
almost all of them successes at the time and capable of arousing
audiences to rapturous enthusiasm whenever and wherever
they were revived thereafter. The achievement of Gilbert and
Sullivan was to replace the hitherto regular importation of
French *opéra bouffe* by a native product which had the essential
qualities for success even at this late stage in Victorian history,
namely of being funny without being vulgar, of being comic
without being coarse, satirical but unwounding, sentimental
without committing the foreign offence of sentimentalising
'affaires' and of delighting audiences with that skill in playing
with words that Victorians in general found so enjoyable.
Sullivan did his best to become a composer of 'serious' music as
well; he wrote an oratorio in 1877, a sacred cantata in 1880, a
Te Deum to be sung at the end of the Boer War, the conclusion
of which he did not live to see, and an unsuccessful grand opera,
Ivanhoe, as well as the traditional tune for the hymn *Onward,
Christian Soldiers*. No doubt he was always uneasy at being, as

a composer of 'comic' opera, entirely without roots in the English musical tradition.

In that melodrama retained much of its hold on the London theatre to the end of the reign it is not altogether true that the stage was divorced from the national culture. The Victorian years were full of melodrama: of village girls seduced, of cruel landlords and lascivious squires, of tiny graves, of domestic and passionate crime, of fortunes suddenly made and as suddenly lost. But as taste was 'refined' and the society play came to predominate along with the frothy nonsense of musical comedy, there is more substance in the charge; indeed, unreality was carried to the heights of glittering absurdity by Wilde himself. But the Victorian music hall was always rooted in the national culture. Its significance lies in its function as a bridge between the less deprived among the lower classes, and the otherwise distant middle and upper classes. But although music halls at the end of the reign were something of a cult among a limited part of the aristocratic and literary worlds and were no longer thought exclusively working class or 'low', they cannot be said ever to have been looked on as really reputable places. They were regarded throughout their history as being in questionable taste and never completely lived down their early reputation as 'unsuitable' for serious-minded, thoughtful people as, in the end, the cinema managed to do. The very intensity with which the legend of 'the halls' was (and is) cultivated suggests a strenuous effort to compensate for their always dubious status even in their heyday. Their great quality was that they were a wholly native institution and that in some degree they succeeded in presenting the working-class people of the British Isles to the rest of society in a warmer and more human way than the social reformers, rescue workers and investigators of the Victorian age could do; and to that extent they lowered, just a little, the barriers that divided class from class in that age. True they bowdlerised themselves on stage and often sentimentalised themselves excessively; but any cultural activity with a wide following that caused metropolitan audiences to feel at one with costermongers from Kennington or with Irish immigrants as well as, in due time, the working class of Lancashire, Yorkshire and the Clyde, was performing a valuable service to the society at large. The halls also spoke for the working classes themselves, deepening their own sense of community, enabling them to laugh in public at their own weaknesses as well as those of the 'swells' and 'toffs' they so frequently burlesqued.

Music halls were evolving and changing all through the Victorian years and were in many ways merely the gradual sophistication of the traditional masculine association of alcohol with singing, yarn-spinning and personal showing-off, all with or without female society but often with the women playing a merely subordinate role. Basically there would seem to have been about 4 'institutional' origins of the later 'halls'. There were, first, the male singing and glee clubs meeting regularly in taverns. Then, there were the Song and Supper Rooms, such as Evans's in King Street, Covent Garden, the Coal Hole in the Strand and the Cider Cellar in Maiden Lane, which provided food, drink and entertainment, vocal and instrumental, into the small hours, and perhaps what were coyly called *tableaux vivants* or *poses plastiques*. Although females were not usually admitted to these entertainments, they were such acknowledged 'night haunts' that they were regularly 'haunted' by street women. The third and more enduring element was the more nearly working-class Tavern which had a licence for the performance of music. Notable Taverns were the Royal Standard in Pimlico (which eventually became the Victoria Palace) and the Robin Hood in Holborn. As well, there were the so-called 'Saloons'; the Eagle Tavern under its alternative name of the Grecian Saloon was one of these, and there were other well-known ones in Whitechapel, Hoxton and Lambeth. These sometimes offered something more approaching genuine theatrical or operatic entertainment for the better-off working class.

The question of which general form these miscellaneous institutions should eventually assume was to some extent the result of the Theatre Act of 1843. Henceforth premises could be licensed to present plays, but not to sell drink in the auditorium, or they could be licensed for drink but not for theatrical performances. This made it fairly certain that most Taverns would opt for the latter alternative as being more remunerative and less uncertain: the Victorian populace could do without stage plays but it could not do without drink. In 1847, 1848 and

The Canterbury Hall, 1856

1849 the first establishments to be referred to as Music Halls were set up, though only one of them was thus designated at the outset. This was the Surrey Music Hall at The Grapes in Southwark Bridge Road, which had previously been known as the Grand Harmonic Hall.

More celebrated, however, was the Canterbury in Upper Marsh, Lambeth, which was first taken over by Charles Morton, an enterprising young licensee of 30, in 1849, and rechristened the Canterbury Hall when in 1852 he opened a hall specially built to house his entertainments. 'Ladies' were admitted to all performances, a break with the previous tradition of allowing them to attend only on special 'Ladies' Nights'. The premises were enlarged at the end of 1856. Admission was 6d (2½p) in the body of the hall in the late 1850s and 9d (4p) in the gallery. The seating capacity was 1,500; the audience was described as consisting chiefly of 'respectable mechanics' and 'small tradesmen with their wives, daughters and sweethearts' with a smattering of 'fast clerks' ('fast', presumably, because they were, for all their low rates of pay, expected to hold themselves aloof from 'mechanics' and 'small tradesmen'). The Canterbury was approved of by upper-class observers as a great improvement on previous establishments of a similar kind: the bas-relief on the wall above the heads of the orchestra was adjudged 'tasteful' and the large number of chandeliers earned the rating 'peculiarly tasteful'. The 'turns' were given on a platform furnished with a grand piano and a harmonium, on which 'interval music' was played. The chairman sat at a table below the platform, rising to announce each new 'turn'.

Within a very short time the success of the Canterbury Hall

led to the establishment, all between 1857 and 1864, of the Middlesex Music Hall in Drury Lane, the Metropolitan Music Hall and the Bedford in Camden Town, which were all developments of pre-existing Taverns and Saloons. In 1861, Morton himself moved to the edge of the West End by opening the Oxford Music Hall on a site at the corner of Tottenham Court Road and Oxford Street, once occupied by the Boar and Castle Inn which dated back to the seventeenth century and on which, in 1926, one of Lyons' Corner House restaurants was built. Famous in Victorian times though the Oxford was, Morton, even before he had managed to open it, had already started another which was to have an even longer history, the London Pavilion.

The character of the halls was much altered first by their popularity, which led to the construction of proscenium and stages in the larger halls, and second by the Act of 1878 which empowered the Metropolitan Board of Works to insist on appropriate standards of building to reduce fire risks. (The Oxford Music Hall was burned out in 1868 and again in 1873.) Both changes worked against the survival of some of the smaller halls: if a proscenium wall was constructed, an iron safety curtain was mandatory and small stages could not take the weight; and the new building standards required finances beyond the means of the smaller operators. Further changes in the 1870s reflected both the official drive towards temperance and the growing popularity of the performers themselves; drinking was first of all relegated to bars at the back of the auditorium, thus providing a promenade for drinking, mingling with the crowd and watching the performance, while the tables in the auditorium were replaced by stalls. Not till the end of the reign was drinking at last confined to bars completely apart from the stage and auditorium. A major sign of these changing times was the complete reconstruction of the London Pavilion at the time of the rebuilding of Piccadilly Circus in 1885. By 1886 the Pavilion did away with tables and the chairman and installed tip-up seats ('numbered and reserved'). In 1900 the interior was rebuilt yet again and 'decorated in the style of Louis xv'.

By the time Edward vii came to the throne the more lavish music halls had become 'Palaces of Variety' and the resort of 'wealth, fashion and *ton*' where could be seen, according to one authority writing in 1895, 'the most prominent and distinguished representatives of art, literature and the law' together with 'city financiers, lights of the sporting and dramatic world and a very liberal sprinkling of the "upper crust", as represented by the golden youth of the period.' Thus the Palace of Variety became the medium by which the wealthy could make contact with talented members of the lower orders of society in a less intimate but also less sleazy way than they had done in the early Victorian years, at the racecourses, the bare-knuckle prize fight and the gambling, cock fighting or ratting den. Little was lost by the change; the relationship was no longer tinged with criminality, even if it was overlaid by a great deal of sentimentality.

The Alhambra, with advertisements, 1899

The last great flare-up about the moral standing of the music hall occurred in 1894 over the scandal of the 'promenade' of the Empire Theatre of Varieties, Leicester Square which was under the management of George Edwardes, and, like the nearby Alhambra (which also had a notorious promenade) was otherwise notable as having preserved interest in the ballet throughout the generation that preceded its return to glory with Diaghilev's 1911 season at Covent Garden. The promenades of both were notorious as resorts of high-class prostitutes: (they had to be high class since the entrance charge was 5s [25p]). A high proportion of the male clientèle of the Empire went there primarily at the very least to mingle with these evidently fascinating, if to modern taste excessively over-fleshed, over-dressed and over-perfumed charmers.

A vigorous attempt was made by a group of courageously high-minded women to get the Empire's licence withdrawn on the double charge that it was a known resort of prostitutes and that the ballet dancers were too scantily clothed. As a result of the agitation, and despite a furious counter-agitation (which included a claim by London cab-drivers that a lucrative element in their business would be imperilled) the London County Council decreed that the promenade be abolished and drinks be no longer sold in full view of the stage. George Edwardes, the manager, therefore constructed the minimum necessary alterations and cut off the promenade and bar from the auditorium by means of canvas screens. These were shortly afterwards pulled down by angry young men, who then paraded through Piccadilly waving portions of the partitions and crying 'Long Live Edwardes'! A group of army cadets from Sandhurst took a prominent part in the proceedings, one of their number being Winston Churchill, who preceded the operations by favouring the applauding promenaders with what he later claimed to have been his first public speech. As a result the partition had to be rebuilt in brick; but in 1894 Edwardes had his licence renewed unconditionally and the promenades, both at the Empire and at the Alhambra, con-tinued until voluntarily closed down in 1916 because at that date they offered too flagrant a temptation to young officers on leave from the Front during the First World War. Both establishments, it is sad to report, appear to have suffered financially as a result.

It is therefore not difficult to understand why music halls, even when decorated in the style of Louis xv and presenting extracts from opera and ballet, were never regarded with approval in the Victorian age. The struggle to make the halls respectable had indeed been fraught with problems. Thus the tale is told that in 1878, at the Holborn Music Hall, a sweep was refused entry because he was 'not properly attired'. Besides, he was told, 'he had no collar'. The sweep was outraged 'Collar? Collar? 'Swelp me, what d'yer take me for—a bloomin' dawg?'

The leading West End Halls were not, however, typical even in the 1890s. There were smaller and less fashionable halls in the West End itself, middle-class halls in the better suburbs and dingier ones in the poorer parts, where the traditional chairman still survived. In many of the lesser halls, a contemporary asserted, audiences were perfectly content with 'dull songs, hoary jokes, stale sentiment and clap-trap patriotism'. This reminder of the poor quality of some music hall entertainment puts in proportion the achievements of the relatively small number of those who succeeded in capturing the loyalty of audiences who would otherwise tend to be phlegmatic, or rowdily inattentive because their major purposes about the place were to do with drink or with women. As the century proceeded, they had to cope with audiences which, though grown increasingly attentive, had become more critical and the readier to greet a poor 'turn' with a glum silence or worse still to 'give him the bird'. It was for this reason that the stars of the halls were so much in demand, not only appearing at several different halls in one evening but also going off to halls in the provinces or to appear in pantomime.

Their triumph was a special example of the highly-developed individualism of the Victorians, since the music hall 'artiste' had, unlike a legitimate actor, no supporting cast, no playwright to create his part for him, no director to tell him how to interpret it; even less could he be virtually created as later cinema stars could be; nor, like his successors a century later in the fields of *vaudeville*, cabaret and 'pop', had he artificial devices for rendering his voice audible in all parts of the theatre. He had nothing but the resources of his own personality. He had to command instant attention and hold it throughout his solitary occupancy of the stage. This required in the first instance a profound if originally largely instinctive understanding of the audience, and a split-second responsiveness to its often unpredictable moods. His chief advantage was that his material, if successful, could be taken from hall to hall and town to town, since before gramophone, cinema, radio and television, it could neither be reproduced nor squandered upon a mass audience in one appearance on a network. Thus he could go a long way with relatively little material. W. B. Fair sang *Tommy Make Room for your Uncle* for 10 years in the 1880s and on occasions in 6 different halls in the same evening; and Katie Lawrence's reputation was made, though she sang other songs, by the never-forgotten *Daisy Bell.*

Once he was a top-of-the-bill name, a star would have the huge advantage of instant, uproarious applause the moment he appeared and wherever he appeared. Many stars were therefore associated with a few songs and some immortalised only one; but the titles of some of these songs such as *A Little Bit off the Top, Ask a Policeman* and *Get your Hair Cut* passed into the vernacular. 'The Great Macdermott' sang 'We don't want to fight but by jingo if we do' during the diplomatic tussle with Russia over the Balkans in 1877 and put 'jingoism' in the dictionaries as a result. Although it is impossible to assess the true quality of the more renowned performers, the evidence provided by those who survived to work in their later years in the twentieth century suggests that uninhibited, large-voiced gusto was one major ingredient. Gusto was certainly the reason for the nationwide success in the 1890s of Lottie Collins' song and dance number *Ta-ra-ra-boom-de-ay.* Another necessary element was heavy sentimentality, as in Tom Costello's *Comrades* ('ever since we were boys, Sharing each other's sorrows, Sharing each other's joys'). Hearty patriotism was also prominent: in 1897, Arthur Reece sang *Sons of the Sea* to indicate to the Germans that though they could build ships they could not possibly 'build the boys of the bulldog breed Who made Old England's name'.

Three outstanding successes of the late Victorian halls were Albert Chevalier, Dan Leno and Marie Lloyd. Chevalier, hailed as 'The Coster Laureate', had begun his career as a straight actor and his technique may have been more sophisticated than that of his contemporaries since his coster songs, though hugely successful, were less raucously delivered than most and a shade more subtle. Dan Leno, the outstanding comedian of the period between 1888 and 1901, was also more versatile than most and possibly more discriminating in his choice of writers and material. He ended his career sensationally. In 1901 he was summoned to entertain the Prince of Wales at Sandringham; shortly afterwards he went mad, and after only a brief recovery died in 1904 aged 43; his funeral was watched by crowds '3 deep for over 3 miles [5 km]'. Since her innumerable admirers, many of them writers of outstanding ability, have never succeeded in conveying it, the quality which made Marie Lloyd a legend beyond all others must be said to be indefinable. One can only conclude that, famous though her songs were, most of their apparently overwhelming effect must have depended on the skill with which she projected them.

Further Reading
R. Mander and J. Mitchenson, *The Theatres of London*, 1963
R. Southern, *The Victorian Theatre*, 1970
M. R. Booth, *English Melodrama*, 1965
R. Mander and J. Mitchenson, *British Music Hall*, 1965
H. Scott, *The Early Doors*, 1946
W. Macqueen Pope, *The Melody Lingers On*, 1947

IX

Passing Shows

Quite apart from the more orthodox traditional entertainment available to persons of wealth at the theatre, opera, museum, art gallery or concert room, Victorian London was rich in the less formal kinds of leisure entertainment it provided. The greatest show of the reign was undoubtedly the Great Exhibition of 1851, which set both a metropolitan and an international fashion for that combination under the same roof of instruction designed to be entertaining and entertainment claiming to be instructive which was so distinctive of the nineteenth century. The prime movers of the scheme were those two earnest, intelligent men, the Prince Consort and Sir Robert Peel. The Prince himself was to the project at once a presiding deity and a popular educator, desiring that the exhibition should be 'a whole world of nature and art collected at the call of the queen of cities—a competition in which every country might have a place and every variety of intelligence its claim and chance of distinction. Nothing great or beautiful or useful, be its native home where it might; not a discovery or invention, however humble or obscure; not a candidate, however lowly his rank, but would obtain admission and be estimated to the full amount of genuine worth'.

The site was to be on the south side of Hyde Park, opposite where the Albert Hall now stands, and it was to be housed in what came to be called the Crystal Palace, though it was not crystal and not a palace, but a gigantic iron and glass conservatory, whose design, by Paxton, the Duke of Devonshire's gardener, was based on that of the conservatory Paxton had already built for the Duke at Chatsworth. It was so large that it could accommodate mature, fully-grown trees and rose tier upon tier with avenues and galleries and vaults of glass. It was nearly 1,900 feet (575 m) long and 100 feet (30 m) high, and enclosed an area of 19 acres (770 a). Its iron framework was painted orange, scarlet and light blue, it was pleasantly flanked by lawns and approached by broad gravelled paths used both by carriages and pedestrians. Opened in May, it attracted an average daily attendance of 43,000, the total attendance by the time it closed in October being over 6 million. The cost was £292,794 and the receipts £506,243. The entrance fee was steadily reduced throughout the period it was open, from an initial charge of £1 down to 1s (5p).

Despite the noisy hostility with which it is not only a metropolitan but also an English tradition to greet any proposal to provide the populace at large with entertainment or instruction, above all when it is not the result of a decision by private commercial enterprise, the Great Exhibition was thus an unqualified success. It did not, as was expected, lead to scenes of violence and disorder nor, in spite of its essential character as an international exhibition, lead to the corruption of English morals by an influx of objectionable foreigners. From all parts of the country, thanks to the main line railways and the cheap excursion trains run by a Mr Thomas Cook, employers sent their employees, farmers sent their farmworkers, schools sent children in droves and the rural clergy sent up parties of parishioners. There was much astonishment at the orderliness of these many thousands of humble visitors, many of whom had never been to London in their lives before. Like the many foreigners who also came, they were over-awed; and it was foolish of Londoners to prejudge the likely behaviour of such people by assuming they would behave like the most degraded of London slum-dwellers or the more riotous habitués of the dancing saloons of the town.

Sobriety was partly ensured by the ban the Prince had placed upon the sale of alcohol; exhausted as they usually were by the spectacle of so many thousands of exhibits, the public were unlikely to be greatly revived by the million or more bottles of lemonade they drank and the slightly smaller number of buns they ate. Indeed, the food provided was so indifferent

The Great Exhibition 1851:
Paxton's 'Crystal Palace'

Great Exhibition interior,
with artistically carved
piano

that the famous chef, Soyer, took over Gore House on the opposite side of the road from the Exhibition and turned it into a restaurant named the Symposium of All Nations. He had a thousand visitors a day, took £12,000 and was heavily out of pocket in spite of the fact.

Apart from a multiplicity of exhibits of manufacturing tools, and of the work of architects, builders, naval architects and small arms manufacturers there were cannons, steam-driven fire engines, ploughs and threshing machines, surgical instruments and clocks, and a demonstration of the newly-invented electric telegraph. There were harmoniums and pianos, ribbons, linens, damasks, ostrich plumes, chintzes, hats, bonnets and corsets, large displays of plate glass and a plethora of pieces of large and small statuary, together with elaborately carved sideboards; there were armchairs, sofas, tablecloths and wellington boots. And, as the Illustrated Catalogue of the Exhibition of the Industry of All Nations noted in its preface, 'it is to the honour of Great Britain that notwithstanding the

173

generous risk incurred by inviting competitors from all the nations of the world—prepared as they had been by long years of successful study and practical experience—the fame of British manufacturers has been augmented by this contest'. It went on, alas, somewhat complacently, to assert that if ever another such competition was to be held, 'British supremacy will be manifested in every branch of Industrial Art'.

The Great Exhibition was famous as the forerunner of similar exhibitions held thereafter in all parts of the world. A second International Exhibition was held in London in South Kensington in 1862, though it was overshadowed by the death of Prince Albert at the end of the preceding year. There was a Colonial and Indian Exhibition in 1886, at which the Queen was greeted at the opening ceremony by the National Anthem (of which the second verse was sung 'in Sanskrit'), an Ode written by Lord Tennyson, a prayer by the Archbishop of Canterbury, and the singing of the Hallelujah Chorus and Home, Sweet Home. The Hallelujah Chorus had also been sung at the opening of the 1851 Exhibition and, together with the rest of Handel's *Messiah*, was sung time and again by huge choirs during the subsequent history of the Crystal Palace as a place of popular resort after its removal to Sydenham, where it remained until destroyed by fire in 1936. The site of the 1862 Exhibition in South Kensington was, out of the money made from the 1851 exhibition, used for the construction of the Victoria and Albert and other museums in that part of London.

The Victorian Londoner's eagerness to combine entertainment and instruction was already being catered for less spectacularly well before 1851. Thus all through Victorian times 'panoramas' and 'dioramas' were popular, indicating that when the cinematograph appeared at the century's end it was satisfying a need as well as creating one. There was Burford's Panorama in Leicester Square (and in the Strand) which would provide exhibitions illustrative of the Coronation, or the sights of Pompeii, Delhi or Sierra Leone. In the year of the Great Exhibition, Wyld's Globe appeared in Leicester Square consisting of four large exhibition rooms which flourished for a decade and provided dioramas of the Australian goldfield, a model of Sebastopol and of anything else that happened to be in the news, usually accompanied by descriptive lectures. A diorama flourished in the Regent's Park from 1823 to 1848, though not with great commercial success. Immense pictures of, for example, Canterbury Cathedral, 80 feet (24 m) long and 40 feet (12 m) high, were exhibited to spectators sealed in a revolving chamber. The most long-enduring of these shows was the Colosseum, also in Regent's Park, a large circular building by Decimus Burton, which had a chequered career from 1826 to 1863 though it was not finally pulled down till 1875. It offered a vast panoramic view of London as seen from the top of St Paul's, had, in addition, a Hall of Mirrors, a Gothic aviary, and a Swiss Chalet from whose windows there was offered a panorama of Mont Blanc. In the 1840s, new attractions included panoramas of Paris and of the Lisbon earthquake.

The Egyptian Hall, in Piccadilly, opposite the southern end of Old Bond Street, was the home of various exhibitions and entertainments. It showed, in 1848, the first panorama actually to move. It exhibited the marvels of the Mississippi, of the Overland route to California, and of the Nile. Large-size pictures were also exhibited there from time to time including, in 1846, two huge canvasses by Benjamin Haydon, one entitled *The Burning of Rome*. More of a draw were General

The Egyptian Hall, Piccadilly, with hansom cabs in the foreground. 'Maskelyne's Magic' was presented here twice daily

Tom Thumb in the same year, descriptions of the Ascent of Mont Blanc in 1852 and a return visit of the Siamese Twins in 1869. The Egyptian Hall became the home of Maskelyne and Cook's magical mysteries, later to become Maskelyne and Devant's, when the Egyptian Hall was transferred to Langham Place in the twentieth century.

Madame Tussaud's waxworks were already a firm favourite. This famous exhibition had an eighteenth-century forerunner, originated by a Mrs Salmon in Aldgate and then transferred to Fleet Street. This show contained 140 waxworks; but in 1812, thieves badly damaged the figures and, although on show until 1831, they were, in that year, sold off to pay the concern's debts. Madame Tussaud started in Paris in 1780, exhibited in the Lyceum Theatre in 1802, and moved thence to the Baker Street Bazaar where, in 1884, the waxworks were housed in the building it occupied till it was gutted by fire in 1925, with the loss of many of its Napoleonic relics.

Pleasure gardens were primarily an eighteenth-century phenomenon and most of them faded away in the early nineteenth. Among those that survived was Highbury Barn, a popular tea-garden resort which obtained a dancing licence in 1856 and drew crowds to its large dancing platform wide open to the sky and lit by lamps. It lost its dancing licence owing to local objectors in 1876 and then closed down. Vauxhall Gardens were in a bad way by the start of the reign and never really recovered from being put up to auction in 1840, though final closure did not come until 1859. By then it had become a raffish caricature of its eighteenth-century self. In the 1850s, its masked balls, which lasted from 11 p.m. until 5 or 6 a.m., were extremely rowdy and frequented by the disreputable. St Peter's Church, Vauxhall, was erected on its site. Its western boundary was where the Southern Region main line now runs immediately north of Vauxhall station and its eastern limit was Oswald Street off Kennington Lane.

More famous in Victorian times were the Cremorne Gardens in Chelsea, just west of Battersea Bridge. From 1832 to 1843 it was chiefly a 'sports stadium' with shooting butts and facilities for golf, but in 1846, under a new manager, T. B. Simpson, it came into its own as a pleasure garden until its closure in 1877. Spread over twelve acres, it had a landing stage for visitors

A Maypole dance beguiles daytime visitors to Cremorne Gardens, 1858

arriving by steamboat. There was usually a large orchestra with a dancing platform around it; it had Swiss chalets, kiosks, temples, a circus, a theatre and a marionette theatre, but still retained a certain rural atmosphere because of its trees. Among its more spectacular stunts was that provided by a Mrs Poitevin who, in 1852, was drawn up into the air by a balloon while seated on a heifer; the law forbade a repetition of this occurrence. In 1861 an intrepid young woman sought to cross the Thames from Cremorne by tightrope, only to discover in midstream that some cad had cut the guy ropes. She descended safely into a boat on the river, only to cripple herself for life shortly afterwards by a fall from the tightrope at Highbury Barn. Another Cremorne stunt man attached to a balloon fell to his death in Sidney Street, Chelsea in 1874.

Usually opened about 3 or 4 o'clock, it was crowded with a mixed clientèle by the evening and it was apparently the rule not to start dancing till after the firework display. When this was over, the more sober-minded and hardworking of the garden's clients went home to get ready for the morrow's work, leaving the late evening to be monopolised by the more leisured of London's young persons. It also had concert rooms, where popular singers performed, and in the 1870s operettas by Offenbach and Auber were presented at Cremorne. Never very fashionable and frequented at best by the middle classes, country cousins up to see the sights, medical students, flash types, or clerks and shop assistants with a roving eye, it was perhaps not quite the haunt of depravity it was sometimes held to be. By the 1870s, however, it had become a rather riotous place, particularly on important race days, Bank Holidays and on Boat Race night.

177

Even so, Cremorne was so various a place that observers
seem to have been able to find there whatever they were
looking for. One observer noted that the difference between
late evening and early evening was not merely that after the
fireworks there was dancing, but that this was the time at
which there arrived at the Gardens 'hansoms freighted with
demure immorality'. The phrase is that of William Acton, a
medical man who devoted much attention to diseases of
women and to the social problems of prostitution from the
1840s to the late 1860s. He found Cremorne disenchanting.
'On and around the platform waltzed, strolled and fed some
thousand souls—perhaps seven hundred of them men of the
upper and middle class, the remainder more or less prostitutes...'
About a hundred couples danced; the rest 'circulated listlessly'
enjoying 'in a grim kind of way' the band and the cool summer
breeze blowing off the river. Lemonade and sherry and the
occasional bitter beer were the principal drinks, but there was
no drunkenness, and the general company barely displayed
'vivacity, much less boisterous disorder'. A party of undergraduates 'were deepening their native dullness . . . with bottled
stout' and some older men 'struggled against depression with
hot grog'. Two 'rosy capitalists' were drinking 'fictitious Möet'
with some fat old dames, 'possibly extinct planets of the Georgian
era'. He noted also that though 'no gentlemanly proposition . . .
would have been rebuffed' the man who waited to be solicited
by any of the women would have to wait in vain. Acton wrote
in a rather self-consciously disillusioned way about Cremorne;
Taine, arriving at 11 p.m. one night in 1872 found the place
packed with people, the men neatly or well dressed and the
women, almost all of whom he seems to have regarded as
prostitutes, also well dressed. The atmosphere was, in his view,
mostly good-natured, but the women's faces were faded and
they were given to occasional shrill screams. He and his
companions were alarmed to find themselves being pinched;
but of the 3 girls for whom they bought drinks, while one was
full of animal spirits, another was a quiet, subdued little
milliner who had a regular lover on Sundays. All three drank
moderately and—apparently—were satisfied to have their
cab fares home paid for them, which hardly suggests an evening
of wild excess or even of great profit.

The Eagle Tavern, with a Grecian Theatre attached to it, in the City Road, was a place of resort from the 1830s until the 1880s. The Grecian Theatre was furnished with the chairs used at William IV's coronation, had allegorical paintings on the walls and boasted an organ and an automatic piano. Outside were ornamental gardens lit by lanterns, decorated by fountains and rendered exciting by the inevitable tightrope walkers. In the first year of the Queen's reign the name Coronation Pleasure Grounds was adopted, the saloon was redecorated, provided with an even larger organ and even ventured into the field of opera, presenting, among others, *The Barber of Seville*. In 1853, the song *Villikins and his Dinah* was first heard there; and under the management of Benjamin Oliver, who preferred to be known as Conquest, the place became famous for some of the best ballet productions in the whole of London. Dancing was a popular attraction and conducted, it is said, with greater decorum than at Vauxhall or Cremorne. There were numerous smaller pleasure gardens of a similar, if less-ambitious sort, in various parts of London in early and mid-Victorian times, for example in Hackney, Chalk Farm, Kentish Town, Kings Cross; and one at Battersea called the Red House which was closed in 1852 on moral grounds and whose site became part of the new Battersea Park. Many of them were open-air adjuncts to popular taverns, others acting as forerunners of the later music halls and palaces of variety.

A famous name in popular entertainment was that of Astley's Circus in the Westminster Bridge Road. Founded in a modest way in 1774, it became The Royal Saloon or Astley's Amphitheatre in 1784, was burnt down in 1794 and again in 1803 and 1841. Thereafter, it was rebuilt to contain an audience of 4,000; and in 1862 Dion Boucicault turned it into The Theatre Royal, Westminster. Apart from Covent Garden and the Italian Opera House, Haymarket, which by 1878 had become Her Majesty's Theatre, there were the Hanover Square Rooms at which the Royal Academy of Music had given its first concert in 1823. It was the scene of performances by Liszt in 1840, and 11-year old Master Antoine Rubinstein in 1842; and Mendelssohn conducted the first English performance of his Wedding March there in 1842 at a concert at which Joachim, at the age of 13, played Beethoven's violin concerto.

THE HOLBORN RESTAURANT

Bill of Fare

→*FOR ❖ THE ❖ GRILL ❖ ROOM.*←

Thursday Evening July 17th, 1884.

SOUPS.	s.	d.
Thick or Clear Turtle	2	6
Mulligatawny	1	0
Consomme with Italian Paste		10

FISH.		
Boiled Salmon and Lobster Sauce ...	1	6
Eels Matelotte	1	0
Whitebait	1	0

ENTREES		
Calf's Head and Piquant Sauce ...	1	8
Pigeon and Peas	1	8
Haricot Ox Tail	1	0

POULTRY.		
Half Duckling	2	0
Half Roast Spring Chicken and Ham	2	0
Pigeon	1	6

ROAST GAME.		
Virginia Quail	1	8

Eating out: Holborn Restaurant menu, 1884, (right), *and a more moderately-priced alternative*

The Prince Consort was a prominent patron of the Hanover Square Rooms, and on occasion selected the programme.

Exeter Hall, otherwise famous as a religious centre, was also much used as a concert hall, chiefly for oratorio. In 1847, Mendelssohn presented *Elijah* there no less than 4 times, once in the presence of the Queen and the Prince Consort. The New Philharmonic Society gave concerts there; Berlioz conducted on some occasions, and 'the Swedish nightingale', Jenny Lind, sang to ecstatically full houses. Exeter Hall Concerts ceased after 1880. At St James's Hall, opened in 1858, most of the great executants of the time performed at the Monday and Saturday Popular Concerts (the 'Pops'); the only problem being that the Christey Minstrels sometimes performed in another part of the building at the same time. The results are said greatly to have disturbed M de Pachmann's performance of Chopin's Preludes.

In the seventies, roller-skating became a sudden craze. Skating rinks were opened all over London, and even the best people took up the sport at the Prince's Club situated where Cadogan Square was later built. The craze disappeared and then reappeared several times, its last short manifestation being at Holland Park Rink in the 1920s. More sinister amusements occupying the borderland between sport and crime continued to flourish well into the middle years of the reign. Bare-knuckle prize-fighting continued; though no longer under royal patronage as in the days of the Prince Regent, it still had aristocratic protection, which made it awkward for the police. A notable prize fight of national interest took place in 1862 between Heen and Sayers in the obscure wastelands of Thames Haven, not far from Tilbury; even at this late period only the most resolute ticket holders retained their tickets, owing to the activities of strong-armed toughs or pick-pockets besieging the station at Fenchurch Street; and so riotous was the occasion that, not even for ready money could the police be prevailed upon to go near the scene. The fight lasted until both men were almost physical wrecks. After that, sparring with gloves came more into fashion as an acceptable sport and the Queensberry rules, devised with the support of the Amateur Athletic Club, at least brought some degree of order and restraint into an otherwise entirely brutal pastime.

Horse-racing was in a hardly less disreputable condition in the early part of the reign and the Derby of 1844 was noteworthy for the fact that 2 of the 3-year olds, one of whom won, were in fact 4-year olds. The matter came before the courts, which took the not unreasonable line that if gentlemen insisted on getting mixed up with blackguards in the business of racing they should take it for granted that they would be swindled. Not until the sixties did racing begin to become less disreputable, but Taine's experiences on Derby Day in 1872 seem greatly to have upset him. In spite of admitting that good humour and gladness abounded and that, here at any rate, the classes mingled, he saw it primarily as a vast, vulgar orgy deriving its spirit from the fact that in England the rich spent so much of their time in the country going about on horseback through the mud, of which he considered the English rural landscape chiefly to consist. He observed that a party of 24 gentlemen proudly flourished the 75 bottles they had drunk between them; that two other parties of 10 gentlemen each got down and started a ten-a-side boxing match; that other gentlemen 'eased themselves' against the side of a carriage full of ladies; and that when a carriage overturned and the ladies fell off it with their legs in the air everybody laughed very heartily. He also claimed to have seen drunks all the way back from Epsom to Hyde Park Corner, reeling about and being sick, without anybody expressing disgust.

It was during the forties that the business of bookmaking first became widespread as a means of enabling more of the population to make bets on horse-racing, a practice which had hitherto been a fairly exclusive activity. Betting shops grew apace, most of their owners being prepared to make a bolt for it if too many favourites got first to the winning post. Since their existence was inimical to the general desire to encourage thrift among the working classes, off-course bookmaking was made illegal in 1853. This at once introduced the bookie's runner but increased the number of bookmakers functioning at the courses themselves. The other aristocratic pastime of gambling at gaming houses also had its imitators in the lower levels of society, but the Gaming Act of 1845 led to the virtual disappearance of gaming on a commercial scale for over a century. It was unfortunate therefore that Edward, Prince of Wales, as a young man was a regular player of baccarat for money.

Similarly in decline were two other savage pastimes: animal-baiting and the spectacle of public hangings. At the beginning of the Queen's reign, cock-fighting, highly organised dog-fights, as well as ratting, at which the object was to wager on a dog's capacity to kill a specified large number of rats within a given period of time, were all in vogue, attracting, like horse-racing, a wide clientèle from the prosperous to the criminal. Cock-fighting was banned in 1849; though surviving in secret in out-of-the-way places ever since, it ceased to be an accepted pastime rather more rapidly than the other brutish games of the early Victorian period. Until hangings in public were ended by an Act of 1868, they were a popular spectacle,

Ratting by gaslight

the size of the crowd depending upon the notoriety of the criminal. At Newgate, more than 30,000 people would assemble on occasion and the crowd did not usually disperse until the body was cut down some 30 minutes after the actual moment (or moments, since the City's hangman was notorious for his incompetence) of execution. As much as £25 might be paid for a room with a good view of a popular Newgate hanging, since, at any rate at the beginning of the reign, it was a spectacle much favoured by certain types of dissolute young men of wealth, doubtless because, even in those days, of its relative rarity. By the 1860s, the more respectable elements had begun to absent themselves, leaving a spectatorship composed, to a large extent, of members of the criminal classes.

The readiness with which certain sections of the wealthy and aristocracy associated with the lower, if not the criminal, or near criminal, elements in society in prize-fighting, horse-racing, cock-fighting and the like, early in the reign, may well have been due to the widening gap between aristocracy and middle class created by the conversion of so many of the latter to the cult of respectability which grew up out of Methodism, Evangelicalism and the doctrine of self-help. The idle, vicious young aristocrat or even the merely exuberant and arrogant members of the aristocracy, whatever their age, had at least this in common with the shady characters they met at prize-fights and race meetings: that they disliked middle-class respectability. The decline of the rowdier and more brutal sports attested to the growing strength of the respectable ideals of the middle class and to the conversion of a major part of the aristocracy to the same ideal.

Another factor contributing to the decline of the cruder as well as the more languid pastimes of the age was the growing interest in organised games from the 1860s onwards. The 1870s

Seeing the lions fed at the Zoo on the first August Bank Holiday.

saw the emergence of the Rugby Union, the Football League and County Cricket Championship. Lawn tennis was invented in the 1870s and in the 1880s came the enduring delights of the safety bicycle. Although lawn tennis soon became primarily a social pastime for the middle and upper classes which, if not necessarily at this stage very atheltic, was usually fairly graceful, the other activities had a wider social appeal, except, perhaps, for Rugby Union, which was always, in London, a minority pursuit. The organisation of games on a national basis was possible only because of the communications revolution achieved by the railways and the use, from 1840 onwards, of the penny post, and it inevitably tended to increase the importance of the capital in this sphere of activity. And wherever earnest young men from public school or university engaged in voluntary social work among the London back streets they were quick to spread the manly skills of 'a good game of footer' and the virtues as well as the technique of the straight bat. The active participation of poor children in organised games was inhibited, however, by the lack of open spaces in the inner areas; and this fact tended to be overlooked by middle-class commentators who, as football in particular became professionalised, accused the working classes of turning the race into a 'nation of spectators'. There was far too little opportunity for the working classes to be anything else in late Victorian London; and the large number of sports grounds which was to develop in the outer suburbs is indicative of the lack of playing space there was in the centre.

There was rather less public pageantry in London during the Victorian period as a whole than might have been expected of the capital city of the richest country in the world and, by the 1880s, of the world's largest empire. During their married life, neither the Queen nor the Prince had much liking for formal display; and when the Prince died it was often only after the most persistent pleadings that the Queen could be persuaded even to open parliament in person. After Albert's death, London's only moment of real excitement was the occasion of the wedding of the Prince of Wales and Princess Alexandra in 1863, from the public celebration of which the Queen kept herself grimly aloof. There was a growth of republicanism which was stemmed only when, at the end of 1871, the Prince of Wales had a serious attack of typhoid. At Gladstone's insistence, there was a service of public thanksgiving for his recovery, held at St Paul's in February 1872, at which the Queen, together with the Prince, were tumultuously cheered. The Queen, in her pernickety fashion, refused firmly to wear her crown and wore a bonnet instead; but also insisted on appearing in an open carriage. If, as Gladstone wanted, she was to show herself in public, she would do the job properly.

There were, after that, three great state occasions in which Londoners participated unreservedly: the Golden Jubilee of 1887, the Diamond Jubilee of 1897 and, in 1901, the Queen's funeral. Although less remembered than the Diamond Jubilee, that of 1887 was a great gathering of European princes and monarchs; the People's Palace was opened by the Queen in the East End, there was a Thanksgiving service at Westminster Abbey, a royal garden party at Buckingham palace and a review of the Volunteers in Hyde Park. Hyde Park was also the scene of a gigantic party for the poor children of London, each of those attending being given milk, a bun and a Jubilee mug. The Diamond Jubilee was a celebration of Empire. When the Queen drove from Buckingham Palace to St Paul's (still declining to wear anything more ostentatious than a bonnet) there were large contingents of troops from all parts of 'the colonies' in the procession so that, perhaps for the first time, Londoners were made aware of how truly their dominion was spread 'over palm and pine'. The service at St Paul's was brief and held on the cathedral steps, since the Queen was much too lame to climb them. In the evening she appeared on the balcony of Buckingham Palace in a wheel chair. It was on this occasion that an unknown member of the cheering crowd is said to have called out 'Go it, old girl'.

Diamond Jubilee procession, Trafalgar Square, 1898

Her funeral in 1901 provided Londoners with a spectacle that combined majesty with awe, though the Queen herself had no great liking for traditional funeral trappings. It was at her command that the streets of the metropolis were hung not with black but with purple cashmere decorated with white satin bows. The crowds lined the route of the funeral procession from Paddington station, under grey skies and in a silence broken only by low murmurs from each section of the crowd as she passed it, and by the whispered sound of the men's removal of their hats or caps as they watched her go by them for the last time. Among the kings and princes who rode behind the coffin, none looked more splendid than her grandson, the German Emperor, within little more than a decade afterwards to become the detested 'Kaiser Bill' of the First World War. The Queen's death was everywhere regarded as the passing of an age. And much had indeed changed in London since the far-off day when, as an 18-year old, the Queen had first worn the crown that now rested on her coffin. But for all that the Metropolis had changed and grown in the years between, too few of its gravest social problems had been solved and even in the newest of suburbs change had nowhere wholly eliminated the past. Never submitted to the will of a dictator, always resistant to the timid pressures of a cautious central government, London remained rich in the fascinating confusions and contrasts of a place where there had been no master-mind to plan, where the new rubbed shoulders with the old-fashioned, the old and the ancient, and where the changing present was everywhere neighbour to the continuing past.

Further Reading
Elizabeth Longford, *Victoria, R.I.*, 1964
E. Beresford Chancellor, *Pleasure Haunts of London*, 1925
Kellow Chesney, *The Victorian Underworld*, 1970
C. Hobhouse, *1851 and the Crystal Palace*, 1950
The Great Exhibition, 1851: The Art Journal Illustrated Catalogue, facsimile reprint, 1970
George Augustus Sala, *Gaslight and Daylight*, 1860.

Index

The numbers in **bold type** refer to pages on which illustrations appear